TELEVISION AND CHILDREN

Roger Singleton-Turner

BBC *Television Training*

First published in 1994
BBC Television Training
BBC Elstree Centre
Clarendon Road
Borehamwood
Hertfordshire

Throughout this booklet the pronoun
'he' should also be taken to refer to 'she'
and vice versa.

General Editor: Gordon Croton

Design and production: Shirley Greenfield

Photographs on pp. 73, 79 and 97 by Sharon Childs

Printed by Able Printing Ltd
Paddock Wood
Kent
England

Title page: *Box of Delights*

Acknowledgments
The author wishes to thank Hilary Shipman Ltd
for their permission to quote from
Television is Good for your Kids
by Dr Máire Messenger Davies.

Contents

INTRODUCTION

'Television and children' is a big subject. Students of sociology spend years writing reams on the effects of television on children and on adults. Much thought is given by advertisers to the young audience, and how it can affect parents' buying patterns. Educationalists despair over, or wonder at the power of TV to educate — or at least to give teachers a respite from their less tractable classes.

There is the whole area of geography — the way programmes travel across the world, giving, so some say, one nation an unhealthy influence over the minds of another. There is the range of opinion on what is and is not suitable for a child audience and the difference between a 'children's programme' and a 'family programme'.

At this time, too, we are at the beginning of a major change in viewing opportunities, with the advent of satellite television, and the spread in Britain of cable TV. There is also great concern about standards of children's programming, and a group called *British Action on Children's Television*, following in the footsteps of the American counterpart, is up and running.

My experience of children's television began as a viewer in 1949 and grew in 1967 as a floor assistant, and later as an assistant floor manager for BBC Television.[1] Since 1974 I have been directing television programmes, first on the storytelling programme *Jackanory*, then on drama series for children which include *Grange Hill*, set in a London comprehensive school, *The Story of the Treasure Seekers*, an adaptation of the late Victorian stories by E. Nesbit and the comedy series *Gruey* and *Gruey Twoey*, I have also directed adaptations of Allan Ahlberg's *Happy Families* stories, the sci-fi comedy thriller *Watt on Earth*, and the all-puppet programmes *Mortimer and Arabel* by Joan and Lizza Aiken. This experience has been entirely with the BBC. The suggestion that I write this book followed a period as an instructor in BBC Television Training.

Because of this background, most of the references in this book are to BBC television programmes and methods, and you may feel there is a bias towards drama-style programmes. This is unavoidable, but I shall try and keep to general principles.

Since sociological research into television viewing habits is not definitive and since there are so many variables in making programmes in any context, and for the reason that this work has to be kept to a manageable length, much of what follows will be a matter of opinion. You may well disagree with what I have to say, but I do urge you to consider the topics I raise — to think as broadly as possible round the subject of your particular project.

This book is designed for those who may wish to work on children's programmes. A certain familiarity with the basic processes of programme making is assumed — if in doubt, there are other books available from BBC Television Training that you may find helpful. Broadly, it deals with that which is special about children's programmes; what differences there are in their making; the subject of morality and children; audience reaction in its broadest sense and future possibilities at a time of rapid change.

WHY MAKE CHILDREN'S PROGRAMMES?

The basic answer to this came up at the launch conference of the British Action on Children's Television Campaign. One parent said she was increasingly angered over continual references to the costs of children's programmes, that they are an investment in the future, and that we must persuade television companies on this subject "... to be philanthropic, because it's worthwhile".

To British audience researchers a child is defined as being aged between 4 and 15 years old. Anyone with a child under four will notice the flaw there. They will also observe that children will start reacting to a TV screen almost as soon as they can focus their eyes, certainly within the first few months of life. Preferences can make themselves felt from around the time a child begins to speak and can be marked by the age of two. Most self-respecting 4-year olds these days will be thoroughly familiar with a wide range of different types of programme, and will have strong likes and dislikes. They will also be able to distinguish between 'commercials' and programmes.

In practice, most BBC children's programmes do not set out to cater for children much over 13-14 years old. By that age, many have developed other interests, and are exploring other entertainments. Many would not like it thought that they watched 'kids' stuff'.

As children mostly have small experience of the world, their terms of reference are different from those of an adult. Their capabilities, mental and physical also, of course, differ from those of an adult. Piaget apparently held the view that children under 12 years of age were incapable of abstract thought. This theory is, I am told, these days not widely held among child psychologists, but the fact that such a theory could gain wide credence at all is indicative of the fact that children do go through phases of readiness to deal with different types of concept. There is overwhelming evidence now that children are not simply open books in which information can be written in any order (as I was taught in the late Fifties), but that their minds are ready for, say, language development at one stage, and high-level physical coordination at another.

It is an observable fact that most children will find quite a lot of adult programming boring, either in content or in presentation. It is also evident, from the way in which film and television shooting and editing techniques have changed and developed over the past ninety-odd years, that response to, and interpretation of, material can be learnt.

In short, in terms of development and subject matter, children can be regarded as a special interest group. Better still, they can be regarded as a group of differing interest groups. As the 4 to15-year olds currently constitute approximately 17% of our population, this makes them a particularly large and worthwhile special interest group. Since the audiences of the most popular BBC children's programmes may reach 7 to 8.5 million, about half of whom are actually children, their 'special interest' productions yield audience figures well in excess of those for some well-regarded adult programmes.

In any case, the young are our future, and demographics and number crunching aside, they deserve the best we can do in the way of tailored entertainment and stimulation. If we short-change our children, then *no one* can expect a fair deal.

Another issue concerns the necessity, or otherwise, for specialist programme makers for children. Because of the different paces and areas of development in children, groups of people have grown up in the television industry who try to respond to these differences. There are people who can do wonders with sticky back plastic or who can become involved in the day to day needs and problems of the likes of Jemima, Hamble, Little Ted[2] and their descendants.

Others, like myself, have discovered a niche, a way of finding children to play the parts of children — not always as straightforward as it sounds — and of making drama featuring children, for children. These should not be confused with films and programmes with children that are an evocation of childhood made for an adult audience.

I would contend that there is a specialist application of television expertise in the making of such programmes. That people can move from making children's to making adults' programmes should not be doubted, but it should also not be doubted that there is a major place for the specialist. If you have any concern for children other than as audience statistics, read on.

NOTES

1. The BBC equivalents of, respectively, call-boy and assistant stage manager.

2. These three were characters (dolls and a teddy bear) on the long-running BBC series for the under fives, *Playschool*.

Chapter One

Children and Television

Blue Peter, 1975

It can be argued that children may have three broad relationships with television:

- Most obviously as viewers — as consumers of the programme 'product'.

- As participants: on 'phone-in programmes; as contributors of letters or paintings, etc; as individuals, talking about their interests or hobbies; as consumers of toys, school dinners and the like; as researchers into environmental problems, and as actors.

- As individuals seeking (or passively imbibing) information.

Looking at that list, it occurs to me that there is one other category — that of the programme maker. Apart from 'Young Film-maker' competitions, there has not been much room on television, as currently constituted, for school-age television producers, camera operators and the like. Time and financial constraints make it easy to see why, but as cameras become cheaper and lighter, with formats such as Hi-8 offering transmittable quality pictures, the floodgates will soon open. (BBC's *Video Diaries* has already begun the process.)

Viewers

Before discussing the way programmes are made for a particular audience, it may be useful to consider that audience and the way it views.

Clearly, there have been many changes in viewing patterns in this country over the past forty or so years (i.e. since the sole UK broadcasting organisation, the BBC, recommenced its Television Service in 1946). Most of the readership of this book will barely remember the time before the availability of colour television and the presence of three channels (at least). British television has moved on from a single monochrome channel transmitting a picture of (by modern standards) dubious quality with a service consisting of *Children's Hour*, followed by a gap, and then two to three hours of television for adults beginning at 8 p.m.

Now we have twenty-four hours of television, the potential, with digital compression, of many more terrestrial channels, and dozens of satellite channels. To all this is added the possibilities of some form of wide screen/high definition system (notwithstanding that 405-line pictures received this appellation over forty years ago) and the widespread use of video recorders. Reports speak of children watching 4 or 5 hours of television a day. This was just not possible within the early lifetimes of those who currently run our television stations — never mind whether desirable or statistically accurate!

Children are exposed to television from the moment they are born — bottle feeding a baby does not allow a massive range of alternative activities. The age at which they start to take a real interest will vary enormously, but toddlers of 18 months may very well become involved in cartoons or other animation programmes like the perennial *Postman Pat*. Some parts of series like *Rainbow* and *Playdays* are also likely to prove attractive. Each child differs and can be attracted to programmes not at all aimed at it. *Neighbours*, is a case in point. This series was made for an adult and family audience. In this country, at the time of writing, it is immensely popular among children of all ages and widely differing backgrounds.

Another aspect of viewing at an early age is the way many small children pick up advertising jingles — and ad-men's messages. If you do not believe this, then you cannot have had the experience in a supermarket of being told by a 5-year old to buy this or that product because it has a 'magic' ingredient which is good for you — or too many E numbers that are not.

Watch with others
A great deal of research has been done on the way children watch television, how they react to it, and what they get from it. If you are interested in making programmes for children, you should, for the good of your soul, watch television with children from time to time.

There are different ways of doing this: join in watching in a household where you yourself are known as part of the furniture, rather than as a special guest. Watch the programme —

notice how well the set is adjusted, how much of the picture disappears into domestic cut-off, especially on the wide-screen sets. Notice how much and how little attention is being paid to what is happening on the screen. Sometimes, a child will be reading, and watching, or dressing a doll and watching, fighting a friend, arguing with a sibling, doing homework, refusing to do a chore, playing with the cat, or any of a huge range of activities. Some of these are clearly incompatible with close attention, some are not. Most will allow a sampling of the programme to take place. That allows the child to keep up with the plot or to reject an item as 'boring', and a surprising amount will be retained even when concentration has apparently been low.

The contrast to this is the child who will watch in rapt attention from the beginning of the opening titles to the last of the closing credits. In fact, of course, that last sentence is misleading — any child is likely to fall into each group at some time, for some programmes.

Attention span
The BBC did not take the pre-school programme *Sesame Street* when it was first offered for a variety of reasons. There had been a lot of research prior to the programme's production about children's reactions. One finding was that the maximum attention span in its target audience was two to three minutes. This led to there being no single item on *Sesame Street* of a length greater than about three minutes. This was compared unfavourably by programme makers at the BBC with the length of commercial breaks. It also went against the attitude that children should be challenged and stimulated; that children never offered longer items would never cope with longer items, and the view that children offered longer items were in fact quite capable of coping with them. This is a variety of having your cake and eating it, but the fact is that some pre-school children (in the UK this means under-fives) can concentrate happily for well over half-an-hour. (I have seen such concen-tration in the theatre for *Peter Pan*. This is not perhaps relevant to television, but it knocks on the head the theory that 'under-fives' cannot concentrate for more minutes than they are aged in years.)

The other aspect of concentration, or lack of it, is absorption of information. This is extremely difficult to measure, since children can be in a position of knowing something empirically, without necessarily recognising it intellectually, and without the ability, perhaps, to articulate their understanding.[1] It is helpful to a child's understanding of a programme if he is watching with an attentive adult, who can fill in any gaps for that particular child.

Cautionary tale
Many years ago, at the height of the interest in space travel, in the lead up to moon landings, a couple of space scientists were being interviewed for a BBC magazine programme. To add an extra ingredient, some bright spark had the brainwave of inviting a class full of children from the local primary school to the studio to ask questions. The questions were, on the whole, not particularly searching, but there was one very dissatisfied customer when he asked the American experts, "How do astronauts eat?"

The answer to the question involved special non-spill packs of food, and explanations about heating and the lack of normal cooking facilities. The boy was obviously not happy, and I could not immediately see why. It occurred to me later, though, from his supplementary question about weightlessness, that what he wanted to know was how it is possible to swallow in weightless conditions if gravity is not there to pull the food into the stomach. The answer he wanted, of course, was a simple explanation of the swallowing mechanism. Unfortunately, as a mere floor assistant, I was not in a position to offer the answer to the boy, nor to offer a prompt to the presenter. The lad may still be wondering.

Numerous examples can be found in talking at length to a small child, or group thereof, of such failures, not of intelligence, not of language, but of time to understand, to think round to a child's eye view of a subject.

Sorting information
On the whole, an adult has many facts and experiences to call on: if a new fact is presented in isolation, there are likely to be

enough other bits of 'old' information available to link this new fact into the mind's system, even if a certain 'calculation from first principles' has to take place. A child does not have this range of experience, and odd facts can end up being joined on to existing experience in the most amazing way. This is not to insult children — it can happen to anybody. Just look at the way that, in the absence of other information, barnacle geese were once supposed to originate from a particular type of barnacle. Again, remember how it was once widely held that the sun went round the Earth. These are examples of adults wrongly integrating, and integrating incomplete, information.

Ways of watching
Watching in the home with children is a good idea — it puts your heart-searching, your blood, sweat and tears into a new perspective — but do not feel that you have to have a child in order to make children's programmes. It is the most inordinately long-winded way of going about audience research. It lacks statistical validity, too. Very few of the total number of 6-year olds in the country are likely to turn to their parents and say, "I do like these opening titles".

It is also possible to go to schools and view tapes with groups of children of assorted ages. This will provide much food for thought, especially once you get the group past, firstly, saying what they think will please you and, secondly, saying what they think will upset you.

Some of the reactions will be fairly predictable, but almost any group will come up with some fresh thoughts. Beware the group effect, though. It is quite possible that a strong feeling will be expressed about a particular topic: other children may then feel disinclined to go against the tide of their peers' opinion — watch the body language, and encourage a differing opinion to emerge. That is when the discussion will take off!

Children on-screen
When children watch children's television, it can be a passive process, but very often it can be shown to be much more. The

primary purpose of children's programming is to entertain. Children come home from school, and may choose to unwind in front of the TV. A degree of 'flopping' may be felt to be justifiable. It is, though, quite possible that the child 'flopped' in front of the television may be stimulated to write in and comment on a programme, to send in a picture or to press for a *Blue Peter* Bring-and-Buy-Sale to be set up at his or her school. (In 1993, 90,000 children wrote in to *Blue Peter* for instructions on how to build a cheap but serviceable copy of the *Thunderbirds'* Tracey Island!)

Children may well be taking on board information presented in a light-hearted way from all kinds of programmes: from *Blue Peter*, the doyen of magazine programmes now into its fourth decade, or from such series as *The Really Wild Show* which may stimulate who knows what interest. It was undoubtedly programmes such as *Look* and *Zoo Quest* (the latter, with David Attenborough) in the Fifties that stimulated my own interest in biology and in television.

There have been shows from the mists of time which exploited this stimulating effect and which have depended on children wanting to contribute. The earliest example I can remember is *All Your Own*, in which children came along and demonstrated their unusual hobbies, or played, danced or sang. At least one 'pop' group, the King Brothers, was launched by its appearances on the series. This programme is now held up as an example of the BBC at its most patronising. As a child viewer, it did not then seem so to me. Styles change.

Even the continuity announcers heard between programmes for many years have been replaced by in-vision presenters who expend a great deal of effort relating to their viewers, who respond handsomely with paintings, letters, cards, and so on.[2]

Schools, cub and brownie troops, clubs and organisations of all sorts volunteer teams for anything from quiz shows to activity games. Such programmes depend totally on child participation. There are series, like *Why don't you (switch off your television and do something less boring instead)?* which do not have even a token adult presence.

There seems to be ample evidence that children like seeing children on television. Sometimes there is the vicarious thrill of wishing to be there, or perhaps of relief at *not* being there if it involves being covered in water, paint or gunge. There is also a critical element — the "I could do better myself" syndrome.

Children do seem to like seeing their peers on the screen, and this may account for the popularity of children's drama featuring children. One child, when asked why, after a day at school, he liked to come home and watch *Grange Hill* responded, "Well, it's nice if it's been a rotten day at school to come home and see someone else getting it in the neck". Perhaps this attitude accounts, too, for the popularity of some adult soap operas.

Children, then, are a part of children's television notwithstanding the restrictions that surround their appearances. Their presence as contributors helps keep you in touch with them as viewers.

Before joining BBC Children's Programmes in 1974, I worked on the output of most other departments. It was only in Children's Programmes that the audience was considered as an individual child (or a group of two or three children), rather than a statistic measured in millions where the ratings game could be played to the full.

Much is talked now of demographics and audience reach, but the principle in Children's Programmes is still that programmes are made, not for the millions, not for other programme makers, but for children. The same approach applies in Schools Television programmes where the audience is the class — and the teacher.

"Back in the office"
We have moved from the time when the bulk of programmes were transmitted live to that of today, where many programmes go through a multiplicity of stages from off-line editing, video effects editing, on-line editing, to some form of sound dubbing. It is easy, therefore, to lose touch with the effect on the audience of the programme you are making.

The viewing of a programme with its producer at the end of the post production stages is quite different, in my experience, from watching the same programme as it is transmitted, in the context of the afternoon's transmissions, when surrounded by a small group of one's colleagues. The points that will occur to your colleagues may very well not be those that occur to your target audience, but they will nonetheless be stimulating. You will probably find your own awareness heightened, too, by watching with an informed and potentially critical group.

Times have changed. This method was perfectly possible when I started out as a director. You need to work in a more or less supportive, stable and confident environment, with other specialist children's programme makers for it to happen. But such groups tend to become fragmented and short contracts have made new directors perhaps less ready to accept criticism from their peers, however well meant.

Another interesting phenomenon is the change in your reactions when watching a recording of your own programme a year or so after its completion and transmission. You will have moved on in your experience and technique, but most of the tensions surrounding the making of the programme will have evaporated. You may well find that you can approach it with a more open mind. You may feel all is well — certainly some of the things that caused you sleepless nights at the time will no longer be a problem, but your views on its pace, let us say, may very well be different.

In writing this, it is assumed that a high proportion of children's programmes are transmitted within the working day, and so are accessible at the 'office'.

It is a good idea to look at a broad range of children's programmes both before you involve yourself in them and while you are making them. This includes the purely educational 'Schools' output and the shows on other channels, cartoons, dramas, and magazine programmes. Fashions change, styles change and unless you exercise care you can end up on a long-running strand, with an old fashioned product. I will return to this topic — I do not believe in change for the sake of it, but

17

change in response to changing needs and circumstances is vital.

Teaching with television

Most children in the U.K. have access to specially made Schools Programmes at school and at home when there are staggered half terms, or when they are away from school for whatever reason.

Many of these programmes stand up on their own. Most are designed to form part of a lesson and depend on the teacher having prepared other notes or material. The success of the programme, how much it is enjoyed, how stimulating it is to the pupils then rests, to an extent, on the effort the teacher applies, and on his own enthusiasm for the programme and the way it deals with its subject. A development in this field is that education has become a bi-media area, with a close integration of radio and television material, as well as printed matter.

Some of the differences between Schools and Children's Programmes could be summarised as follows:

1) The bulk of those viewing a Schools Programme do so in a controlled environment. Children there are not left alone — except in unusual circumstances — to watch.

2) Such programmes can afford to be stimulating, even provocative, since there will be a teacher on hand to sort out individual queries and, one hopes, to guide a balanced discussion afterwards.

3) In the making of a Schools Programme it should be possible to think of a fairly precisely defined age group or ability range. In Children's Programmes, we think in terms, say, of 5-7 or 8-12 year olds; Schools Programmes would probably be more precise, and talk of "a first year course".

4) Schools Programmes which deal with sociological issues and English frequently use language stronger than would be countenanced on Children's Programmes, and may deal with violence in a tougher way, too.

5) At the other end of their spectrum, they overlap with Children's Programmes output with such series as *Picture Box, Words and Pictures* and *You and Me*. The main difference, here, seems to be in the speed of delivery. More time is left for response on, say, *Words and Pictures* or *Let's read with Basil Brush*, than would usually be allowed on Children's Programmes. Of course, a group of twenty or thirty children will respond more slowly than a child alone — who is likely to respond internally, rather than vocally, if at all. Perhaps there are more distractions at home, too: perhaps the child viewer would 'zap' to another channel, given half a chance.

6) Programmes for schools are planned to tie in to ever-evolving syllabus systems, and to current educational theories about child development.

7) The making of the programmes has to be linked to the publication of programme notes and other material which may require verbatim accuracy. This may prove a problem if the text has already gone to press before the programme is shot.

8) Each programme is likely to be used for four or five years[3] so minor points, like the use of extremes of fashion, need to be carefully considered.

9) Many programmes for schools these days take advantage of the fact that most schools use video-recorders. Programmes may be designed to be viewed in sections, allowing 'junctions' where the taped programme may be switched off for discussion. Again, with any taped programme, it is easy to go back over a section to check anything that is unclear, or to check the accuracy of the recall of the viewers.

Children's Programmes are designed to be viewed at one sitting. Schools can be licensed for the taping of educational material. It is also increasingly likely that educational programmes will often be transmitted at night, with the specific aim of being taped for later use.

Incidentally, I am aware that the programmes mentioned in this book are a complete mixture of 'historical', 'present', and those that are no longer made, but which the reader is likely to remember — if he or she spent childhood years in Britain.

NOTES

1. This rash statement is based on my own memories, intuition, and conversations with children — and on the cautionary tale that follows.

2. This is actually a return to the in-vision and youthful presenter convention of the late Forties and early Fifties. I remember Jennifer Gay from my early childhood. Other channels change their styles, too, and have tried in-vision presenters. The BBC has a major advantage, because of its still (more or less) unified structure.

3. For many years Actors Equity, the actors' union, had an agreement with the BBC that governed frequency of repeats, and the period in which they could be shown without special re-negotiation. This deal also covered the number of 'out of time repeats' permitted in any given year. The agreement for Schools Programmes was slightly different. In the current climate, the tendency is to create a variety of deals which should be far more flexible and will take account of the many ways now available of distributing programmes.

Chapter Two

Making
Programmes for Children

Grange Hill, 1980

When I told my head of department, Anna Home, that I was writing this book, she was, initially, surprised. Her comment was that there is no difference in making programmes for children and in making them for adults. She is, of course, quite right. The techniques, the visual vocabulary, the resources, the equipment, the processes are all the same.

The difference, however, lies in the varied ability of the different age groups within the audience to understand the common vocabulary and grammar of the medium.

The second difference lies in the terms of reference that will be understood by different sections of the audience. The general knowledge of my generation covers different topics from the general knowledge of current schoolchildren. At ten years of age I could have told you something of British history in terms of kings and queens; I would immediately have understood 'the war' to refer to the Second World War. I would not have understood the words 'feminism', 'environmental issues' nor even 'gay' in the ways they are understood now by at least some 10-year olds.

For example, reference in one of my programme scripts to a Black Maria went over the head, not merely of my own daughter, but also that of the assistant videotape editor in his twenties. The age gap beween the generations shows itself in such subtle ways.

However, Anna Home's comment on the making of children's programmes is also important in another way. The standards of applied skills, the budgets and the care and attention provided in children's programmes should all be at least as high as those provided for adult programmes. Children have neither economic nor political power, but they deserve the best we can do for them.

AGE

Just as children develop their use of language and visual perception in a measurable way, so their ability to cope with images on television will vary. There are two aspects to this:

- Developmental psychology

- Television grammar

Developmental psychology
As children develop they go through the stages of learning to focus their eyes, of recognising faces and other objects. They will learn that an object can be viewed from many angles yet still be the same object. They will learn the difference between the object and a picture of the object, and that the object can be pictured in many different ways — from a simple line drawing to a full-colour photograph.

They will learn to respond to sounds, to recognise individual voices, to understand tones of the same voice, and eventually to understand words. Further on, they start to use words and make up complex sentences.

This may all seem pretty obvious, but it does have a bearing on your programmes. A child may watch almost anything on television, but a young child, lacking the equipment to interpret images as fully as an adult is likely to lose the thread of a narrative and to create extraordinary constructions in his mind to explain what he has seen.

There is ample evidence that children may even be confused by the juxtaposition of a medium or long-shot of an object with a close-up. Specifically, it has been shown that a child may interpret two such shots as showing two different sizes of object.[1]

The whole grammar of television needs to be learnt by each viewer. There is evidence that the language of film and television is learnt in a similar way to spoken language and that children of increasing maturity accept with understanding an increasing vocabulary of filmic conventions.

Even the zoom and the unmotivated pan need to be used with care in programmes for the young. Since neither camera facility is one natural to the eye, both should be used with care on any programme. The brain has to learn how to interpret and update the image as it changes.

Criticism has been made of panning and zooming on still pictures. Once a child has reached six or seven years old, however, she can probably cope with such devices without loss of concentration, but, if your programme is aimed at the very young, consider hard what you are trying to achieve with such camera devices.

Research[2] shows that the way information is absorbed is affected by the way pictures are cut to words. This is what you would expect, but it might not be so apparent that adults and children of different ages differ in the way they accept information, as the criteria for cutting are changed.

There is no simple way of summarising years of research by large numbers of experts, and I have already stated the limitations of my own experience. In spite of that, a common sense approach that seems to be backed up by research might go something like this:

- The younger your audience, the more straightforward should be your approach. E.g. Keep shots uncluttered, show objects clearly, avoid too fast a cutting rate and be careful not to edit out too much 'real time'.

- Avoid zooms and unmotivated pans. Rather, allow presenters freedom to move in relation to a relatively still camera, with a relatively static field-size.[3]

- Children of school age appear to understand sequences where action has been edited out, e.g. in a montage, but they need to learn the conventions. Be aware that the impact of the montage may not be the one you intend!

- Keep a sense of scale (this is a point all directors should keep in mind). You can have no idea of the size of a teddy-bear in the absence of a known object within the same shot for comparison — and I do not mean a foot-rule: the presenter, or part thereof, would be more helpful to give this sense of scale.

- Do not assume the ability to make logical leaps — each step in a chain of action and reaction needs to be represented — and in its right place — if you are not to confuse at least part of your audience.

- Do not display two sets of conflicting information simultaneously. That is, avoid words saying one thing whilst the picture is showing something else (e.g. the presenter is showing in close-up how to measure ingredients for a cake, and at the same time is telling the audience where to write for a recipe sheet. This works on *Food and Drink*, but not, probably, on programmes for younger viewers — even supposing them capable of writing in themselves.)

- Keep the language straightforward. I do not mean 'talk down' to your audience, nor do I mean avoid long words, but try to keep your presenters to the point and to speak in simply structured sentences without too many clauses. However, remember that many children love playing with words and like the chance to use new ones, so beware of the danger of using impoverished language.

Obviously, the higher the age of your target audience, the further you can go towards a more complex televisual vocabulary and the tricks used in some adult entertainment. Never forget, though, the likely spread in the age range of your audience and be prepared to make allowances for this — or accept the consequences of puzzling, and perhaps therefore boring, some of your viewers. (On the other hand, do not be afraid to use effects to construct an image or to create 'magic'. In these cases, clearly, the digital effects should be transparent, technically, so the picture should not appear to be treated.) It is difficult to maintain a reasonable balance of all these factors.

Further considerations
Children vary quite as much as any other group of people. Even from birth their individuality shows up — ask any parent.

This being the case, the capacity of individuals in any given age group will vary considerably. This obviously affects which individual children a programme will attract and therefore the size of your audience.

Other factors are involved here (apart from the attractions of rival channels and videos), such as the time of day the programme is shown and the time of year (how often did you stay in at the age of nine to watch television on a hot afternoon in August?). Preferences can also be shown to vary with sex and socio-economic grouping. Boys and girls develop at different rates and, whatever those wishing for interchangeability between the sexes may say, they show different preferences. (How many small boys chose to watch *My Little Pony,* and how many little girls liked *Teenage Mutant Hero Turtles*?).

The socio-economic divides are more difficult to define, but, the statistics tell us, they are there. It is probably simpler to think in terms of the way the experiences of a child watching on the eighteenth storey of a block of flats by the M6 in Birmingham, will differ from those of an otherwise similar child watching on the eighteenth floor of a block of flats in the Barbican, London.

SUITABILITY

Statistics suggest that 98% of homes in Britain have at least one television, and about 60% of homes where there are children also have a video recorder. It is predicted that, by the year 2000, about 30% of homes in the U.K. will be able to receive cable or satellite channels. Approximately 30% of homes have one or more children under 15 years of age.

It is said that children watch too much television, and that television is bad for them. In fact, some statistics show that children watch less television than adults by several hours a week.

Current research seems to suggest that children themselves treat television in a variety of ways: it provides common ground for chat, an easy source of entertainment and a source of information. Other research,[4] suggests that "*watching television does not turn children into zombies*". This evidence indicates that children who read or take part in other activities do so *whether or not* they have a television available. Those who do not already have a wide range of other interests, do not seem to develop them *even if* they are deprived of television.

Children are undoubtedly stimulated by television and are introduced to many things that would otherwise be outside their experience. This can, of course, be a problem if the concepts are introduced in a disturbing way, or if there is no adult on hand to clarify, or if there is an exhortation to imitation which could be followed by disaster.

In a drama series for children from Thames Television (at that time an independent franchise holder in the London area), *Pressgang*, dealt with a 'child reporter' following up a case where a boy had jumped to his death from the top of a block of flats while under the influence of solvent abuse. *Grange Hill* has also had characters under the influence of drink and drugs, and there have been incidents shown of girls shoplifting. One early episode showed a boy falling to his death from a multi-storey car park, following a 'dare'. There have been at least two other depicted deaths in dubious circumstances over the years. The 1991 season fully discussed the consequences of a teenage pregnancy at the school (a storyline followed up with the schoolgirl mother in the following year).

Interestingly, the discussion within the programme was mainly concerning consequences and courses of action. The 'morality' of the event seems not to be an issue. In spite of this, the audience reactions seem to have been generally favourable.

All these items were liable to rouse 'Angry of Amersham' to write and complain. Some of these items would have simply puzzled younger children, and some would certainly have distressed part of the audience.

Of course, there are those who call for outright censorship, and equally those who call for 'the frontiers of television to be pushed further back'. As with anything else, acceptable fashion varies from year to year and from place to place. So what are you to do?

The short answer is simply to consider the possible consequences of almost any physical act you show, or imply, and be aware of outlooks other than your own. Each individual will interpret events on screen with reference to their own experiences, no matter what signals and signposts you include.

Yet most (but not all) the research again suggests that children do develop a 'pre-teen' recognition of the different levels of realism on television, both in terms of the difference between fact and fiction, and between different types of drama. Further, the emotions generated by one programme can be altered by the programme following which may well be something completely different.

Children do tend to watch more than one programme at a time. This is why it is important to view your own programme on transmission and in the context of an afternoon's entertainment. This, indeed, is precisely what producers and directors in the BBC have to do from time to time in preparation for an informal — but no holds barred — discussion within Children's Programmes. Such meetings always produce an interesting debate, and can be salutary and of great use.

Language
There is a generally accepted view that there is nothing to be gained by allowing the use in Children's Programmes of 'bad language'. This means in practice that no obscenity or blasphemy may be used, and that most other expletives would also be deleted. 'Bleeding', for example, is not used, except literally. The euphemism 'ruddy' (except as meaning 'of a reddish hue') is also discouraged. Words that are corruptions of blasphemies, such as 'Crikey', 'Cripes', and so on, have also been known to provoke public reaction, so are not encouraged. In practice, the time you spend trying to justify the use of such words is better used to more constructive ends.

Paradoxically, it is worthwhile to be acquainted with a good range of such words, so that they do not take you unawares

— an example in this category might be 'pillock', which I have seen removed from more than one children's script where it had been allowed to enter through ignorance. I am still awaiting reaction to — and a hidden meaning of — the word 'Wazzock', which we used in *Gruey* and *Gruey Twoey* with some frequency, but only after checking slang dictionaries, and local children, for double meanings.[5]

There is, of course, a classic BBC tape which reveals both the problem and possible ramifications from the radio series *Music and Movement*, where a very straight-voiced presenter asks her audience to take out their balls and throw them in the air. Doubtless a case *of honi soit qui mal y pense*. But the producer, so the story goes, was warned of the double meaning, refused to recognise it, and the story has caused great hilarity ever since.

People of a nervous disposition
What of 'matters of a disturbing nature?' At the time *Grange Hill* introduced the subject of shoplifting, one headteacher wrote in our defence that children were able to work through difficult situations in their minds while watching our programmes, and so they would be less likely to be railroaded into taking part in something they would later regret. This, too, was my hope as we shot the sequence. (Is it, on the other hand, significant that the bystanders in the location shopping precinct in South London were willing to offer practical tips on how this 'nicking' should be done?).

I was told years later that there had been cases of shoplifting apparently inspired by that particular sequence. And yet the reaction from 10 and 12-year olds to other events suggests that equally they can be shown the futility and unattractiveness of such proceedings — and their consequences.

There are, of course, serious problems in reaching definitive conclusions about the effects of television. The BBC stopped showing adults smoking (except in very negative circumstances — and then only after much heart searching) before most of today's audience for children's programmes was born. Even on adult programmes, fewer characters were shown to be smokers. Statistics on the deleterious effects of smoking have been around for many years, and these effects have been well publicised by television, as well as the other media. Nevertheless, smoking among the young in this country is actually on the increase. What conclusion can we draw from this — apart from the obvious one that the road to Hell is paved with good intentions?

Violence

There are many things that the older generation of television directors would not show in children's programmes even now: deliberate blows to the head (although this is allowed in the *BBC Producers Guidelines*, providing that the serious conse-quences of such an act are also made clear),[5] hiding in derelict car-boots or refrigerators, the holding of a knife close to the throat, and so on. The prime concern is to minimise the possibility of imitation, but there is an element wishing not to distress those of 'a nervous disposition'.

Personally, I would not wish to show violence in such a way as to make it seem desirable to use it, or to make it seem 'fun' or 'exciting'. It is perfectly possible to use the device of Greek tragedy and show the consequences of violence, while limiting the violence itself to something that happens off screen.

Because the audience is so varied and so fragmented, it is impossible to gauge the effects of any given scene on any given part of it. Each child will have his or her own level of development or readiness to cope with violence, with death and other difficult matters, and we have to be aware of this in making material for such an audience.

It is clear that many parents do not like the thought of their children being exposed to television violence. It is not an appropriate response from programme makers that such con-cerns are 'only from the parents', implying that therefore they are of no significance. (This is a view that has been accepted by more than one programme maker.) Unless we are certain of the effects of, say, violence in what we produce, I believe we should err on the side of caution.

Over-protection?

In contrast to these thoughts is the desire not to coddle, not to over-protect. Death occurs in the best regulated families. It the one certainty in which we all share, and it seems to me helpful for television to accept it as a fact of life. The American series *Sesame Street* dealt very sensitively with the subject when one of their elderly actors died.[6] Another series, this time from the BBC, *Dodgem*, centred on a boy coping with life while his father was undergoing a mental breakdown following the death of the boy's mother in dubious circumstances. Both of these seem right and proper.

I would advocate a frank view of death, but not, on the other hand, scenes of naked passion on children's television. For a start, such matters are not spectator sports, and the sexual development of a child is so personal to that child and her own circumstances that any unsolicited 'help' from television is as likely to be confusing as not, unless there happens to be an adult prepared to back up, expand and interpret the pro-gramme makers' intention.

These two sections indicate, I hope, the conflicts and difficul-ties there can be in making programmes. Most of the time, though, it should be possible to entertain, stimulate and inform children without promoting anti-social behaviour.

Anti-social behaviour

This raises the question of how to define 'anti-social beha-viour'. In addition to the issues already raised, it might be considered offensive to show a child getting away with bullying, or simply using a sneering tone of voice to an adult. *Grange Hill*, for instance, has been criticised for the way it shows the children speaking to the teachers. Teachers, on the other hand, frequently say how true to life most of the children are and then complain about the way we show teachers. On the other hand, many adults say they knew teachers just like the ones we depict. Yet other teachers say that the incidents shown are too tame by comparison with real life.

One way around some of the problems might be to 'flag' material with difficult or more-than-usually-frightening content with an announcement at the start of such a programme. At least then the viewers could not say they had not been warned. Even this would not help late tuners, nor would it help the lonely 5-year old.

Another answer might be to put programmes for slightly older children on the air at a later time and on a different channel — assuming that your television organisation has that option. At the time of writing, the BBC has two terrestrial television channels, which has enabled such a solution to be tried out with series like *Tucker's Luck* and *Maggie*. Unfortunately, a lack of funds prevented the experiment being prolonged by the BBC during the Eighties. Now we have the prospect of making 'teenage' programmes again, like *100%*. It will be interesting to see how they develop in contrast to 'Youth' programming.

Conclusions

Firstly, it is a truism that you cannot please all of the people all of the time.

The second is that you can be wrong even when you are right. *Jackanory* once had a story concerning the ghost of Sir Walter Raleigh. Mention of the Bloody Tower (at the Tower of London) provoked at least three 'phone calls to the duty office about bad language.

The third conclusion is that there are many things that can offend — genuinely, and that can cause distress — genuinely.

All the programme maker can do is to be as sensitive as possible, right down the line — to try and put negative thoughts into a positive attitude and to have a considered reason for showing distressing subjects.

There are things that are, perhaps, not best dealt with by a children's programme. What these things are is best assessed in the light of your personal culture and experience, but this, of course, will identify with only a part of the audience. For a start, the programme makers are likely to be at least ten years older than most of them!

It is far better that the programme maker should be able to take a responsible line for himself, than that a body of censors should take that line for him. In any case, nothing ruins a programme faster than an editorial committee.

People do have a responsibility for their own lives and for those of their children. Parents and children must therefore reach some sort of understanding about how their television sets, video recorders and satellite dishes are to be used. We do not make programmes for parents. We should not make programmes for parents. But I believe we have a responsibility to parents for what we feed to their children, just as much as schools have an obligation to consider the effects and quality of what they provide for school dinners.

Even then, with everything considered, with the best will in the world, misunderstandings will occur. Even a bright 6-year old might be confused by the News, and ask if those dead bodies are really only actors. (And an equally bright 7-year old will be under no illusions whatever.)

The nine-o'clock barrier
It has been the custom to keep the more violent and the more sexually explicit films and (even) News coverage until most younger children have gone to bed. The time at which this is deemed to have happened is 9 p.m. This code has been accepted by both the BBC and the Independent companies.

There are only two flaws. One is that very many young children — remarkably young, sometimes — do stay up beyond this watershed. The other is that programmes accepted as family entertainment do show gore and (at least) implied violence before that time. *Casualty*, the BBC series set in the Accident and Emergency department of a general hospital, had its transmission time changed temporarily because of the violence within it, and there is guaranteed unpleasantness twice a week in Albert Square, the home of the soap opera, *East-Enders*, not to mention the sex, violence, and general nastiness of the James Bond films which are shown regularly, especially on Bank Holidays, beginning before 9 p.m.

As a maker of children's programmes, it is well to remember what your audience is likely to be seeing outside special children's slots. Demographic breakdowns on this topic make interesting reading.

NOTES

1. For a simple and readable expansion of this, see *Television is good for your Kids*, by Dr. Máire Messenger Davies, published by Hilary Shipman Ltd.

2. Once again by Dr. Messenger Davies, with Dr. Colin Berry and Brian Clifford.

3. A motivated pan would be one in which the camera panned, following a person's move across the set, or following a hand pointing from one object to another.

4. Which was quoted by Dr. Barrie Gunter in an article in *The Guardian* newspaper of April 15th 1991. There are more thoughts on the subject of language in *Matters of Public Concern* on p.136.

5. For a further discussion of this subject, see p.136, *Matters of Public Concern.*

6. On the subject of 'the elderly', it also seems right and proper to me that television presenters should represent more of a cross section of society than they currently seem to. Not everybody is a whizz-bang 22 year-old, and most children have grandparents.

Chapter Three

Writing for Children

Five Children and It

The best programmes in any field of television are always the ones that have the best scripts.

But what about programmes that depend on ad-libbing, chat shows, quiz shows and the less formal magazine programmes?

The answer is that they all have a format and a structure. They all have some sort of presenter or presentation team. If the format is inherently a good one and if the presenters are good at ad-libbing, at responding to guests, participants and each other, then the probability is that the show will be both good and popular.

This popularity may be undermined if the show, however good in itself, becomes swamped by too many others of similar nature, however good they each are in their own right. Thus a games show is devalued if there are too many on every other channel.

Facets of 'good', or at least popular shows, can also become devalued by excessive imitation: I have heard a few children speak with irritation at the way gunge seems to appear in all children's games shows.

Obviously, if the show is a drama or a documentary it will have a script. It may have been written well in advance of recording, or it may (especially with a documentary) evolve as shooting takes place.[1] However the final result is arrived at, the word is as important as the picture in terms of transmitting information from you, the programme maker to the viewer.

So far as writing scripts for children is concerned, there has been much excellent work done over the past four or five decades of British children's television. The single central question it may be necessary to ask is if the subject matter is 'fit' for children.

One aspect of 'fitness' concerns the conditions under which viewing is likely to take place. The BBC still draws the distinction between 'Schools' and 'Children's' television. This distinction is not always appreciated by the general public, nor even by government ministers in the Department of Education and Science. It is sometimes not appreciated even by those working within the television industry.

What you consider 'suitable for children' depends very much on your point of view. Much also depends on the timing of the programme and its transmission context. Nobody, for instance, would have expected the long running series from Thames Television, *Rainbow*, to deal with childbirth, except in the context of a 'happy arrival'. Yet daytime programmes like that are sometimes followed by detailed discussions on childbirth, the traumas thereof and other topics supposed, perhaps, to be above the heads of any children still watching.

Many programmes regarded as eminently suitable for small children are placed in the first hour or so of Children's BBC. At about 5 p.m., on most weekdays *Newsround* is transmitted, a straightforward news-for-children programme, that deals with anything and everything that may crop up in the main news an hour later. (It has even 'scooped' items before the later bulletin.) There has been much discussion over the years about how much detail we should show of war, starving children and of disasters generally, whether man-made, man-induced or natural.

The BBC has been running *Newsround* (formerly called *John Craven's Newsround* after its first presenter) and *Newsround Extra* since 1972. The fact that these programmes have dealt with most of the major news items since they started demonstrates that it is possible to cover almost any topic, however sensitive, even if it follows the mildest of material.

There is regular debate within the *Newsround* production team about the stories they should be covering, and the way such stories are presented. They are very careful to give a run-down of the background to major stories, assuming no particular prior knowledge in their audience, and also to select carefully which pictures and which aspects of the story are given most weight. Even in the midst of the Gulf War and the action in former Yugoslavia, they covered the major developments, no

37

matter how bloody. Their approach tends to be straightforward, unspeculative and as uncomplicated as the matter will allow.

In the context of 'difficult' subjects, it is worth noting that *Newsround* maintains a steady audience, if the BARB figures are any guide. On the subject of popularity, it is worth noting that one programme in the BBC documentary series, *The Lowdown*, produced by Eric Rowan, gained the largest audience of children (among children's programmes) for a particular week. Its subject was a girl who has had chemotherapy and two operations for a brain tumour and who has produced a book to help other children about to go into hospital. Tough subjects can achieve big audiences!

There are, in general, two schools of thought about suitability:

- Children's Programmes should be a "safe haven", a secure place in a world already sufficiently insecure.

- Children should not be deceived about the world and what it is really like. They are about to inherit it.

The trick is to get the balance between these two right. Personally, I think children should be allowed to be children, they 'grow up soon enough'. On the other hand, I want my own child to grow up aware of the world around her. If subjects are sensitively handled, children can gain a great deal from television.

I believe, with the reservations already expressed, that children do take from what they see that which they can handle.

All children eventually want to know, for instance, where babies come from. The answer to the first query should be simple and short — the child will demand more information if it is not satisfied. What it does not want, first time around, is an entire course in gynæcology and obstetrics! It is perhaps advisable, therefore, to structure programmes containing 'difficult' material in such a way that information is not forced on those not yet ready for it. This brings us back to the writing, and an understanding of the way in which pictures can be put together with words to intensify, and to soften, a particular point.

After *Newsround*, the BBC currently shows a variety of programmes, like *Grange Hill* and other dramas, from the children's classic, *Five Children and It* to *Country Boy*, which dealt with an unscrupulous businessman causing havoc through uncaring pollution of the environment. This series included the poisoning of the boy hero and the death of his dog.

Five Children and It (first shown on BBC *Children's Hour* in 1951 and re-adapted in 1991) concerns five Edwardian children and their adventures following the granting of wishes by an ancient, grumpy hypochondriac of a sand fairy. It had good viewing figures and was popular with a wide cross-section of children.

This popularity resulted in a sequel being written for the BBC by Helen Cresswell, *The Return of the Psammead*. There clearly is still a demand for that style of drama, as well as more 'relevant' and 'challenging' contemporary material.

Country Boy, on the other hand, dealt with topical issues, and was very much a story of the Eighties. It went out in the same slot as *Five Children and It*, that is 5.05 p.m. on a winter Wednesday afternoon. In spite of its modernity, it was nothing like as popular. This cannot wholly have been due to parental influence, to those who remembered the book and the earlier production of *Five Children and It*. Perhaps it was due, simply, to children not liking so much a story based largely on such a major 'issue'. Perhaps the audience was taking from what was on offer only what it wanted.

Whilst no-one can deny that the environment is high on the list of concerns of large numbers of children (as well as adults) throughout the nation, it may be that the interests of children *vis-à-vis* entertainment change more slowly than television producers think they do. After all, a good story is a good story, no matter when it was written. There is a great stock of good stories written in the past already known to you and me, perhaps, but fresh and new to a child.

There is, on the other hand, a sense of alienation among some sections of the audience for the 'period piece', and there is a continuing debate as to whether E. Nesbit is an author we should be promoting in the 1990s. My own feeling is that a good story, well presented, will work whenever it is set and whenever it was written.

The Return of the Psammead was a clever sequel to the original, keeping very much to Nesbit's own style — and period.

In contrast to this is *Maid Marian and her Merry Men*, a development of the Robin Hood story by writer and performer Tony Robinson and director David Bell. These series were set loosely in the 12th century (but with many anachronisms), and were popular both with children and adults — especially members of BAFTA.[2]

As programme makers we need to be aware of what is likely to be attractive to children now. We need to avoid the trap of giving today's audience that which pleased us 15 or 40 years ago. We need to resist the inclination to stick to modern stories because we might think that 'children cannot relate to the past'. (I think most children, whilst not being budding historians, have some curiosity about what has gone before.) Above all, we need to resist the economic pressures *against* doing a period drama because period drama is particularly expensive. The visualisation of period that is inherent in such a production is surely helpful in showing children the way things were, that 'this' is not how things have to be, nor how they will necessarily remain. In other words, period drama can provide a thundering good story and can be informative as well as entertaining.

It is worth noting that such dramas, whilst expensive, are all popular among children. A glance through the Top Tens of specially-made children's programmes of the last year or so, shows a very high proportion of dramas and surprisingly few cartoons. There may be half-a-dozen dramas in the Top Ten, one or two *Blue Peters*, a couple of others like *Hartbeat* or *The Really Wild Show*, and perhaps only *The Disney Club* and one other cartoon. However, this may not hold true for the future.

If the range of the 'glance' is extended to include *all* programmes watched by children, then the effect remains marked. 'Soaps', other dramas, and the odd cartoon, plus assorted 'adults' programmes (sitcoms and games shows) predominate. The programmes that appear in this list usually do not have child-attractive material in opposition on the other channels. There are those who take some of these facts and from them argue that there is no need for special programmes for children. There are also those who say that children's programmes are the best thing on television.

Security
The issue of 'security' of transmission has been under discussion for years. Over the years, children's programmes have been dropped, shifted or curtailed at short notice for news items and sporting events, and other unpredictabilities. Biddy Baxter[3] always fought tooth and nail to make sure that *Blue Peter* went out at its proper time and from a proper (i.e. full-sized) studio. There were occasions on which her programme was the only live transmission to be screened in a more-or-less normal form in the face of industrial action affecting the rest of the BBC output. That was dedication. It was done to avoid disappointing children — to provide a little security.

Whether she was right to be thus concerned, whether children need or benefit from that sort of security is, perhaps, now a matter for debate.

Type of programme
Apart from the time of transmission, that which may be acceptable in one type of programme may not be in another for the same audience. It is obviously appropriate to show the problems of a fat boy sympathetically — for instance, those of Roland in *Grange Hill* — but I would take issue with the producer who once showed a jokey song and dance featuring his normally-proportioned presenter dressed up as the fattest man in the world. The fact that the man was not likely to see the show is no defence.

Equally relevant is food abuse. Viewers of childrens television have been objecting for several years now to food being wasted in television programmes. Dropping large quantities of baked beans all over someone taking part in any sort of television programme aroused strong protests — which is perhaps why 'gunge' was invented. 'Custard pies' seem to be acceptable if they are made from some form of soap foam, but this unfortunately stings the eyes.

The objection stems from the degree of starvation in many parts of the world: if children are prompted by what they see on their television sets to raise funds to help the hungry, they are not likely to take kindly to the apparent waste of food on those same television sets. Saying that the food was past its sell-by date does not cut much ice.

In order to avoid offending the audience, the programme maker needs a very high level of sensitivity. I differentiate between 'offending' the audience, deliberately or otherwise, and 'stimulating them' or 'causing them to think'. It would be difficult to make a programme that had thought-provoking effects or one that was in any sense cathartic, without upsetting someone, somewhere. Just look before you leap.

NOTES

1. There are other types of programme, such as the live drama series, written overnight to the viewers orders, called *It's Your Story*.

2. The British Academy of Film and Television Arts.

3. Biddy was for many years editor of *Blue Peter*, the longest-running children's magazine programme in the U.K.

Chapter Four

Resources

Chronicles of Narnia — The Lion, the Witch and the Wardrobe
on location in Scotland

The early years

The history and evolution of children's television is a book in its own right,[1] but it might be worth a quick glance at how things got to their present state, since there are people who, in the name of economy, seem to be trying to put the clock back.

The BBC began its service for children about seventy years ago, with special radio programmes. There were occasional programmes for children when the Television Service began in 1936. It was natural, therefore, that there should be a place for children in the schedules when transmissions began again in 1946 after the War. From those years, specifically 1949 to the mid-Fifties, I recall the in-vision children's presenter, Jennifer Gay; programmes like the magazine-style *Children's Newsreel*; comedy programmes with Richard Hearne (Mr. Pastry), Peter Butterworth, Mr. Turnip and Humphrey Lestocq; puppet shows with Annette Mills (with Prudence Kitten and Muffin the Mule); *All Your Own*; and drama series which included *The Story of the Treasure Seekers*,[2] *The Secret Garden* and *The Gordon Honour*. There were also dramatisations of fairy tales, and nature programmes with George Cansdale, Peter Scott, David Attenborough, and others. The mixed diet also included the shadow puppets of Hans and Lotte Reiniger, animations like *Captain Pugwash* and so on. *Andy Pandy, The Flowerpot Men, Toytown* and stories from *Rubovia* all used marionettes, which have mostly fallen from favour to be replaced by hand and rod puppets following the lessons learned from *The Muppets*. (The explosion in true cartoons did not seem to begin before Hanna Barbera's *Huckleberry Hound* and *Yogi Bear* hit the British screens.)

Television gradually expanded, its transmission hours grew longer, ITV opened in 1955 and the gap between children's programmes (ending at 6 p.m.) and the evening schedule (by this time starting at about 7.00 p.m.) closed in 1957.

BBC Children's Programmes as a department vanished in 1963, being replaced in 1964 by the Family Programmes Unit. *Blue Peter* continued on the course it had begun in 1958. *Playschool* began and had the distinction, through a power cut on BBC2's opening night, of being the first scheduled pro

Blue Peter, 1971

gramme to appear on the new channel, also in 1964, while the same year saw the introduction of *Vision On*. This programme opened up to a wider audience ideas that had begun on the BBC series for deaf children.

At that period, much of the rest of the material shown in Children's time was supplied by Purchased Programmes, Drama Department and even Light Entertainment, who were responsible for the long-running *Crackerjack*. The parent departments did not employ specialist 'children's' staff, although there were programme makers like Sean Sutton and Dorothea Brooking who had been members of the old department, and to whom we owe a great deal for children's drama over the years.

In the meantime, ITV were doing very nicely for children, with *The Adventures of Robin Hood*, *Zoo Time* with Desmond Morris, a series hosted by Jimmy Hanley, and others like

Thunderbirds (which has recently enjoyed a revival, with an amazing amount of merchandising) and many dramas including an adaptation by Southern Television of *The Lion, the Witch and the Wardrobe*, and many, many more.

BBC Children's Programmes as a department in its own right was reconstituted in 1967 with Monica Sims as its head.

When the people on *Playschool* thought it would be a good idea to expand the story-telling part of the programme, *Jackanory* was born. From the beginning, this programme used different methods to illustrate its stories: drawn pictures, photo-captions, even filmed sequences, with and without actuality sound. It was a small step[3] in logic, then, to do a live action drama — *Joe and the Gladiator* was the first. Others followed, and eventually Drama Department stopped its weekday drama slot for children entirely. Other units evolved, too, *Playschool* spawned *Playaway* and a whole host of other 'light entertainments', the documentaries followed naturally in the wake of the *Blue Peter Special Assignments* and *Newsround*.

It is interesting, also, that there has been a continuity of staff and, to some degree, presenters in children's television. Desmond Morris, David Attenborough and Johnny Morris and Tony Hart have long careers in television, firmly based on programmes for children. Composer performers Paul Reade and Jonathan Cohen were setting out in children's television as I started my work for the BBC. Others have come and gone, but the list of people who began in television by entertaining children is interesting and impressive.

Obviously, this brief summary misses out many of the steps and it would be difficult to say always what was truly a 'first'. *Blue Peter* itself followed directly in the footsteps of the series from the Fifties called *Studio E* (because it was made in Studio E at Lime Grove).

Saturday mornings evolved from a mishmash of cartoons and cheap, oft-repeated, foreign drama to the immensely popular *Multi-Coloured Swap Shop* and its successors. The truth is that each step forward, each new programme, has meant a struggle for resources and cash. Compromises have had to be made, for instance, by making two series shorter than planned and making a third on the difference.

Only when one expansion has been shown to be viable has the next move been allowed. Throughout its history, childrens programming on both channels in the U.K. has been diverse and made to a high standard by people who cared about the particular audience.

Cost-effectiveness

Because of the influences of 'market forces', many programme makers feel their output is under threat, whether in Children's Programmes or elsewhere. Good quality programmes are labour intensive and each one needs to be hand crafted. If the return on any given programme in the commercial world is insufficient to make a profit, then that programme will not survive. In March 1989, David Elstein of Thames Television said, at the Launch Conference of the BAC TV,[4] that children's programmes on ITV and Channel 4 brought in about 6% of the advertising revenue, yet they cost 20% of their expenditure. Under IBA rules the ITV companies had to make and transmit children's programmes. With de-regulation, and with the formation of the ITC to replace the IBA, it was feared that this would cease to be the case. Lobbying of Parliament and pressure from groups like BAC TV meant that the final bill did make the holding of a franchise conditional, in part, on the provision of suitable programming for children. Competition for us at the BBC and the stimulus that competition builds are therefore assured. We hope. Time will tell.

There are programmes on satellite and cable for children, but there appears to be little money available, even now, to provide much new challenging material for this audience. Even the arrival by satellite of the Disney Channel is unlikely to bring new British material to a British audience. One set of figures just before British Satellite Broadcasting was absorbed by Sky Television suggested plans to spend £5,000 per hour on making programmes. This meant they would not have been originating much variety of material, when even an inde-

47

pendent producer at that time would be working hard to make a drama series at £75,000 per half-hour episode.

On 15th April 1991, Alan Horrox, then Controller of Children's and Education Programmes for Thames Television wrote a second article for *The Guardian* with John Hambley, Chief Executive of Cosgrove Hall Productions.[5] In 1990 ITV companies spent £37 million on children's programmes, compared with £35 million by the BBC. They pointed out that Thames TV alone spent £18 million of this. In the wake of the Broadcasting Act's enshrining "of children's programmes as one of its few

Jackanory 3000, The Hobbit, 1979
Bernard Cribbins, Maurice Denham, David Wood and Jan Francis

mandatory categories after 1992", the budget for children's programmes for ITV in 1991 was declared to be £40 million. Perhaps our fears are groundless.

Since 1991, the market has been changing fast. Children's programmes are being shown on BBC's World Service satellite channel, and UK Gold is devouring repeat series from both ITV and the BBC. The Children's Channel has continued to supply cable and satellite equipped homes with its programmes. The Family Channel began operations in 1993, which will give a new challenge to specialist makers of children's programmes. The change in the law that forces the BBC to take a minimum of 25% Independent productions has brought a massive reduction in the BBC's workforce and resource base. Producer Choice opens up the means by which programmes are made, and it is difficult to predict where any given sector of the industry will be in even a couple of years' time.

The practice of pre-selling a programme idea is gaining momentum. This puts an emphasis on packaging, on treatments, and on finding two minutes of good material to show to a range of international prospective clients. I cannot see that the system allows for much that is risky or adventurous. I cannot see, either, that this will encourage the development of an idea or format over two or more series. This is something the BBC has historically done well in many fields. The commitment to carry on the tradition, at least in Children's Programmes, remains. I hope it will continue. With pre-selling there is also the danger that each potential client may wish to remove or water down a specific element in the concept. Since international tastes and susceptibilities vary, the final result could be harmless but bland.

As the revenues for the BBC from Licence Fees have peaked, and as radio and television services have broadened, the whole Corporation has had to become more cost conscious. Nowhere is this more true than in Children's Programmes. Added to this pressure are the massive changes that have followed de-regulation. The BBC had, historically, been able to keep salaries of staff low relative to the main network companies and several other sectors of the industry, in exchange for job security and, significantly, the prospect of working on 'quality' programmes (q.v.). The concept of job security (i.e. a job for life) has disappeared. Paradoxically, the pay of some workers in production has become relatively good, partly from a desire to keep 'key' staff and, partly, because the massive increase in uncertainty and unemployment in the business has forced down pay elsewhere. Nonetheless funds, still so closely linked to the index-linked Licence Fee, are being spread ever more thinly. There are more programmes being produced in factory conditions, especially in the area of games shows.

Faced with harsh economic decisions and in view of the necessary drop in its audience share, given increased choice, I think it is possible that the BBC may still find it has to cut down on its current very large commitment to Children's Programmes. This would be a shame, since, as has been argued very well elsewhere,[6] the needs of the child audience differ from those of an adult audience. Furthermore, much of the output of organisations such as The Disney Channel is aimed at a family audience and not at the differing needs of the different age groups of children.

It has to be said that the commitment to continue is still in place, there is no sign yet of any plan to cut back on Children's Programmes output. The pressures on budgets are real, however, and there is a feeling around that 'something's gotta give'. If the BBC reduced its children's output, it would become more difficult for ITV to carry on its commitment in this area.

The history of children's programmes also could tell many tales of under-funding, of under-dressed sets, of schedules so tight that filmed scenes were under-shot, of the use of a less than minimal number of extras, of little-known actors playing major parts badly (and, it must be said, other little known actors being 'discovered' and doing terribly well). There was even a time when drama sequences were shot on location without the aid of location caterers! I have been fortunate and have not had to work in such conditions, yet. Colleagues in the Independent area have been given schedules that were inconsistent with maintaining quality and remaining inside the law. This problem applies particularly where children are present as actors — of which more later.

Underfunding

There are ways of saving money, but the equation is not simply monetary. Children have access to much of the adult output, to feature films, to videos (not all of them suitable for children, but that is another story) and to commercials. Of the latter, some have a budget greater than a producer of Childrens Programmes for a whole series. Children become used to sumptuous sets, large numbers of extras, spectacular stunts and effects, to a 'zappy' style of editing and so on. If productions shot specially for them do not match up where appropriate, they will feel short changed and turn off.

I believe that while material for children's programmes should be chosen for a specific audience and, while text may be edited so that the larger crowd scenes and most expensive effects are avoided, in other respects shows of a similar type should bear comparison in 'production values' whatever their area of origination.

As for location catering, the cost is great, but so are the benefits, mainly in time saved. A lunch hour can truly take 60 minutes without losing a further hour driving to and from a pub or restaurant that may or may not be expecting you. Artists do not have to change out of awkward make-up or costumes, you do not lose precious shooting time with children and, if conditions are cold and wet, you *do* have a ready and plentiful supply of hot drinks and food. The crew also appreciate the location facility, especially those who arrive first for setting and rigging. The morale and goodwill factors are also not without their significance!

It is clearly commonsense to avoid waste and the spending of money just because it is available. What is of concern is the attitude that can allow an idea to be developed and scripts to be written, with a budget that is totally restrictive — even nonsensical. A quality programme with a drama element cannot be achieved without the appropriate amount of rehearsal time — both 'outside' and in the studio. Fitting a good idea to

51

an inappropriate budget is a crazy way to make anything from tea-cosies to TV programmes.

It follows also that over-zealous use of economic limits may preclude, say, the presence of a 'grips' with a dolly and track on a location as a matter of course. Today's producers and directors are encouraged to use such facilities on a day-by-day basis, having them only when needed. This sounds fine, until you have to adapt your schedule 'on the run' to meet changing circumstances. It is all too easy then to 'make do'. If you make do once, you may be expected to do so again. Fluidity is gradually eroded, spontaneous changes of idea — as part of the creative process, not as mere whim — become impossible. You are on the slippery slope to sloppy programmes. And this scenario is most likely to hit the less prestigious, the less money-generating areas, first. These are my concerns for the future. At the moment, those who manage Children's Programmes understand and resist these pressures and the crunch has not come — yet.

Children's hours
There are complex rules and regulations in the U.K. concerning the hours of work allowed for children under school leaving age (i.e. the sixteenth birthday, or a little later, depending on the time of year). These rules are embodied in the Children and Young Persons Acts, 1933 and 1963, and the Children (Performance) Regulations of 1968 which give inspectors from the local Education Authority the power to remove a child from its place of work — in some circumstances this could mean the closing down of a production. Interpretations of the regulations do vary from Authority to Authority, but the variations are in the child's interest, not the production's, so it is essential that all members of the team are very clear in their minds about what is or is not permitted when production begins. At present, the maximum amount of time a child can work in one day is $3\frac{1}{2}$ hours, as long as he is 13 or over, and these hours can be in a length of day up to 12 hours,[7] if the child is 12 or over. The maximum possible period for continuous work is 1 hour and there are regulations about the length of break between two periods of work, as well. Children under 13 have tighter limits.

Also, 13-16 year olds can perform (as opposed to rehearse) on only 80 days a year, 12-year olds and under, for a maximum of only 40 days. The way that the days are counted is an arcane art in itself. The BBC has its own Code of Practice called *Children in Productions*, which gives the essence of the Acts and offers good advice on the organising of children in productions.

At the time of writing legislation from the European Community will probably supersede the British Acts. The main projected difference is likely to be that anyone under 18 would require a licence.

In practice, therefore, a child can work for no more than half a standard working day. If your project features a single child in virtually every scene, or even the same small group in almost every scene, then 3 minutes a day of cut footage begins to look less than generous. The ideal, perhaps, is to have a contained location and two or perhaps three groups of children 'boxing and coxing'. To all intents and purposes, this is how *Grange Hill* works.

Obviously, there are ways to improve matters: you can employ stand-ins to enable you to line up shots and to read-in out of vision lines, and you can plan meticulously (you must plan meticulously) to take advantage of every scene that does not involve your principal child or children. Unfortunately, the trouble with stand-ins is that they have to be rehearsed too, that changes to moves have to be worked out afresh with the actual child actors, and that the children do not do exactly what the stand-ins do. The usefulness — or otherwise — of stand-ins is something you have to decide in the context of your particular circumstances. These people may be children working under the same rules as your 'stars' or small adults who would normally be employed as walk-ons. (The disadvantage of using children as stand-ins is that there may be friction with the 'real' cast. The problem with walk-ons is that they want to appear in their own right.)

Whatever you do, you will still have to alter your pace of working to suit the abilities of the particular children involved.

It is possible to book an actor and agree his fee at very short notice, but it is not desirable. Most actors prefer time to think about what they are doing and different possible approaches to the part, costumes need fitting, make-up needs designing, and so on. In emergencies, however, you can find actors at 24 hours notice (especially if they are the right size to fit a pre-existing costume). And this does happen — after all, what else can be done if someone is badly injured or taken ill the day before a shoot begins?

Licences

Children are different. If you are working with any child for more than 4 days, or any child who will have to miss any time at school, that child needs to be licensed.[8] The period that Local Authorities need for this process is generally three weeks before the date of the first performance. If you work for the BBC, the BBC needs its own period of a further three weeks, making six weeks from the point of decision, to the point at which you can begin shooting. If there is even the hint of a problem, it is advisable to allow that time before the date of first rehearsal.

There are specially printed forms that have to be completed in order to obtain a licence. There are sections to be completed by the child's parents, the school and the employer. The application must be accompanied by passport style photographs and a birth certificate, or a copy. Provision also has to be made for each licensed child to be medically examined before a licence can be issued. A Local Authority is perfectly entitled to turn down an application if the arrangements are not satisfactory or if the child is not physically fit, or if it is felt that the child will suffer academically. The school has to agree to the arrangements and so do the parents.

When the licence finally does arrive (and this can happen very close to the first performance date if the Local Authorities are hard pressed), a copy of it must be available at the place of work for the inspector (if one arrives) to inspect.

The Local Authority will ultimately need a return of the precise hours of work and tuition at the workplace and at school of each and every child. It is a big job and involves a considerable amount of paperwork.

Finding children

Given that children are not, on the whole, as versatile as adults, you will probably need to see more children at auditions than you will adults. For major parts, where a series stands or falls on the performance of a child, I try and see about 50 children for each one cast. This is the case if there are several children in the story. If there is only one such part, I would be prepared to see proportionally more (American feature film makers sometimes go to extreme lengths, holding dozens of open auditions, in dozens of cities.)

The sum of all this is that programmes with children may need considerably longer in the setting-up stage than an equivalent all-adult production.

Chronicles of Narnia

So, you need more time to find children and more time to shoot them. As for post-production, if you have a number of children, editing may take a little longer than an all-adult production.

A typical conversation with an editor might go as follows:

"John was better on take one".

"Yes, but Mary had that great look on take three".

"But Craig was hopeless, he was best on take two".

So you end up using bits of all three takes. This happens less (or at least, less seriously) with most adult sequences, which are consequently usually quicker to edit. Obviously the more edits there are, the longer the dubbing is likely to take. These subtleties are not always apparent on location and, even if they were, it would not be practical to keep on retaking shots until John, Mary and Craig all did a perfect take at the same time. There is definitely a law of diminishing returns. The trick is to sense when you have everything necessary to make the scene work well and then to move on.

Scripts

Adult actors can generally say with some sort of conviction almost anything that is put in front of them. Most children cannot. If a writer comes from Liverpool, he may write dialogue with Liverpudlian speech rhythms, which is fine, unless the piece calls for London children. Slang and current usage may vary, too, from the writer's preconceptions. The piece may seem as though it is fitting for 10-11 year olds, as *Gruey*, the comedy drama series, did to us.

When it comes to auditions, though, you may find that the particular age group is struggling with the sense or the subtleties of the dialogue. In the case of *Gruey*, which was written by Martin Riley, a writer resident in Leeds, I found two things. One was that 9, 10, and 11-year olds and most 12-year olds, just could not get any life into the scripts, whereas 13 and 14-year olds could. The other was that children to the North and East of Manchester coped with the speech rhythms without

Chronicles of Narnia

difficulty, whereas those to the South and West seemed less happy. The accents of the opposite sides of the Pennines are different, but they seem to have more in common with each other than with the south-western areas of Manchester, which lean perhaps towards Liverpool?

Eventually, we cast children mostly from Bolton and Oldham. But why if the scripts were written for Leeds, use children from Bolton? The answer is economy. Children from Leeds would have had to stay in Manchester for the rehearsal and studio recording period, meaning not only higher 'hotel' costs but also that they would have missed most of a term at their own schools and would have had to be tutored each day. We would also have missed out on the performance of Kieran O'Brien (from Oldham). He was not my initial image of Gruey, but I found it difficult, after two series, to imagine anyone else playing the part. He, incidentally, was one of the child actors who could offer two or more convincing interpretations of one line and who was consistent from take to take. They do exist!

Kieran is now a young adult, still in the business. I forecast that he will do well — most child actors fail to make this transition. Most children, I suspect, are chosen because they are extremely good at being themselves in front of the camera, whilst saying someone else's lines.

Big money!

Of course, there are dramas made for children that do have big budgets — the serial *The Box of Delights* was one. That cost over a million pounds. (Part of this was accounted for by the star catching chicken-pox at the wrong moment.)

To follow the undoubted success of that series, there were *The Chronicles of Narnia*. This is a sequence of four of C.S.Lewis's books set in the mythical land of Narnia. Both projects depended on heavy investment from co-producers. Both were adaptations of books regarded as children's classics.   Both

Box of Delights

required the visualisation of strange creatures and made extensive use of electronic effects. Indeed, were it not for developments in the field of digital video effects in the Eighties, it is doubtful if either series could have been made. The costs of the two projects, had they been mounted entirely on film, would have been prohibitive even for an organisation like the BBC.

It is doubtful whether an equivalent amount of money (bearing in mind the changes in the costing system) will again be forthcoming for making such large scale children's television series.[9]

Studio-based drama
In the Eighties, studio-based drama dwindled in quantity and significance. There are indications that there may be a resurgence because it can be cheaper than location work. In the meantime, situation comedies and children's drama (within the BBC) have been the main areas, where multi-camera disciplines are fully used.

The resurgence is only partial. Few directors now are thoroughly grounded in the use of a multi-camera studio, and many of the most experienced camera operators and vision mixers in this field are past or approaching retirement. The big studio dramas have all the accoutrements, but tend to use one camera at a time.

NOTES

1. The BBC book, *Into the Box of Delights* by Anna Home covers precisely this subject.

2. I saw and enjoyed this version, directed by Dorothea Brooking, which influenced me somewhat when I came to direct the 'remake' in 1981.

3. Actually it was quite a big step. Dramas need much greater funds and resources than a basic *Jackanory*, and the staff concerned did not then have television drama experience.

4. British Action for Children's Television.

5. Cosgrove Hall Productions specialise in high-quality animation such as the popular series based on *Wind in the Willows*.

6. *Television is good for your Kids* by Dr. Máire Messenger Davies. I really do recommend your reading this book as well!

7. This is true only if the child has no other work that week! Beware!

8. If in doubt always check with the appropriate Education Authority — not just the school. There is often an Educational Welfare Officer on whose desk these queries usually land. In practice, you can use unlicensed children for up to 4 days, perhaps at weekends or in school holidays.

9. I have also heard similar fears expressed about the future possibility of making further hugely expensive (but successful) series like *Brideshead Revisited* made by Granada Television.

Chapter Five

Presenters, Content and Style

Hartbeat

Presenters

Once you have got your scripts and format right, the presenters and actors are the next aspect of the programme to consider. They are the ones the audience sees, they are the ones who look foolish if something goes wrong, and they are the ones the audience love (or hate). The director, the producer, and the rest of the people whose names appear on the credits barely exist in the minds of the vast majority of your audience.

It is true that the presenter can take over to an unwarranted extent. There is certainly little point in sending a presenter to Florida, or to Morocco, or even to Caernarvon, if he is only going to make silly jokes under the guise of an interview and thus insult the intelligence — not to say the curiosity — of his audience. In this context, it is interesting to watch Tony Hart on *Take Hart* and *Hartbeat*. He has been working in children's programmes for around forty years. He is popular in the U.K. and abroad, and his programmes on art out-rate many cartoons. Yet he always seems to come across as interested in what he is doing and in the person he is talking to. The subject is the centre of the programme, not 'the personality'. Yet he is very, very far from interchangeable with any one else.

It is interesting that on *Jackanory*, which ranks for actors with *Desert Island Discs*[1] as being a 'thing to have done', the choice of storyteller is not simply a matter of choosing a brilliant actor, or a 'personality'. The trick is to get someone who may be a good actor, who may be able to do lots of different voices, but who has a warmth and charm that filters past the prompting screen, past the camera into the homes of the viewers. How do you tell whether a person has this quality or not? There is no infallible way, but seeing the actor being himself on screen, perhaps being interviewed, is one guide. A screen test is another way. Then there is, of course, instinct.

When it comes to selecting actors to act, that is very much a matter of personal preferences. Some do not have much sympathy with children, or with children's programmes. Maybe their profile is still not high enough! There are many who are fine with children and who have no objection to the type of output, but who may not like the sort of scripts that are on offer

— which is another reason for getting the best possible material to start with.

Content

There is little that cannot be tackled for children *somehow*, especially if you are prepared for a large amount of correspondence. The main points to remember are that the content must be geared to your target age group, whatever the subject, and that those subjects will be most interesting that have some relevance to that group.

If you gear everything to the obvious, then your programmes will be boring. If you allow yourself to be carried away on some esoteric flight of fancy, you will probably lose your audience, as they will be watching without *your* particular terms of reference. If, on the other hand, there is a 'peg' on which to hang your subject, there is a better chance of catching the interest not only of your audience, but also of your commissioning editor, or the equivalent. Your own burning enthusiasm for the project is a major factor, but is not, on its own, enough.

Let us suppose you are fascinated by Admiral Lord Nelson and devise a programme about him. You will do better with the idea if its transmission can be linked to some sort of anniversary of his birth, death, or one of his famous battles, or maybe to an event, such as the proposed demolition of his flagship, *The Victory*, to make way for a fast food fish and chip outlet. (In this case, you would also have to be prepared to answer those critics who felt such a subject to be too militaristic for children.) There is a 'time' for certain projects. By next winter the topic may be dead. To a large extent, therefore, it is a matter of tuning your sensitivities to what people are beginning to think about, so that your programme hits the screen just at the time to catch the particular tide. It is a bit like subjects opening and closing at dinner parties. It is no good thinking of the perfect response to a comment when you are on the way home!

Any experience of working with, or looking after children, will give you some idea of the problems and joys of communication with that particular age group, and of what it is that is likely to catch their interest.

63

Do not forget programmes you enjoyed as a child. On no account try to reproduce them, but try and think what you found attractive at ten, or at five, or even what you liked last night. It may be worthwhile to consider why some adult programmes are particularly attractive to children and to distil this particularity and bring it to your area of influence.

More importantly, perhaps, analyse what bored you and what seemed condescending. The value of such an exercise is that the use of such an approach as *part* of your method, may help you to make a programme that you yourself like.

Since children are a particular audience, it is also important to remember that they have a different perspective on television from adults. The fact that *Blue Peter* has run the 'tortoise hibernating/re-emerging' story for as long as it has had a tortoise is boring — for me. To a child, to whom a year is a long time, such an item is a timely reminder, or a point of familiarity. To an 8-year old, one year represents 12.5% of life.

Once again, there is a conflict. On the one hand, items or stories may be told in their right place every year, or perhaps every couple of years. On the other hand, this does not mean that such repeated items (and stories) should be the same each time. A fresh director, fresh presenter (or actor) should be given their chance to bring a fresh approach each time the item (or story) is done.

There are general points in shooting factual material for children. The experience of one of *Blue Peter's* directors, Alex Leger, whose brain I picked, suggests that you should show clearly whatever it is that your presenter is talking about, almost to the point of not talking about anything you cannot see. Keep things — and people moving. A static head-and-shoulders shot of the presenter talking straight to camera is less visually engaging than the presenter walking along and talking in front of, say, the tree or the steam-engine that is the subject of the programme or item.

Shooting a piece to camera and covering the script in cutaways is a cop-out (or the emergency way out in disastrous weather conditions). Get the presenter involved — see her making things happen. Above all make sure that this question (if relevant) is answered: How does it work?

Avoid too much discussion of abstracts like emotions, unless they are descriptions of how exciting, sad or interesting an experience was for the presenter him or herself.

Do not overdo 'mood' or background music, perhaps even avoid using music sequences that last more than half a minute.

All these guidelines (for they are no more than that) are aimed at holding your audience's attention and making things clear, accessible to the child and stimulating enough to make the child stay tuned. These days it is all too easy to zap around the channels.

Style

This leads back to points made earlier. Our audience evolves at its own rate and, arguably, does not require change at the same rate as adults. The corniest of corny jokes can strike freshly at a child's sense of humour. A child of nine might well have reached that age without being aware that the "leaning tower of Pisa really does lean".[2] Whilst avoiding clichés and the easy way out, of repeating something you did two years ago, you need to develop an eye for what is fresh and wonderful for a child and of not being afraid to tackle again the subject you first tackled two years ago. This is another of the balancing acts you need to perform regularly when making programmes for children.

Another balancing act concerns the use of perceptually salient features, which are defined by Dr Máire Messenger Davies in *Television is good for your Kids:*

"... aspects of a TV programme (or, indeed, of any event) which make people sit up and take notice, because of their intensity, their movement, their novelty or their incongruity. On television, they include physical activity, rapid cutting, scene changes, special effects and sound features... [It can be argued that] at first, very young children's attention

65

is influenced primarily by such noticeable 'formal' features, but that as they get older, children learn to expect that features like the changes of scene, or loud music should be associated with meaningful developments in plot or content".[3]

The lesson is that such devices have to be used with care to avoid raising false expectations in your audience. If used properly, they will certainly help your audience to stay with your train of thought and to understand it.

It follows that however visually interesting 'Pop promo' methods may be to adults, they do not necessarily help younger children to understand the meaning of a song. (In

Happy Families — a rare example of integrated casting

some cases, this may be just as well.) Flashy, noisy presentation of programmes, with lots of graphics, showing messages tangential to the rest of the pictures and the sound track are unlikely to add to the sum of children's understanding, no matter how thrilling they are for people in 'the Business'.

It is also worth remembering the effect that different cutting rates have on different age groups.[4]

The age of seven appears to be something of a turning point in terms of perceptions. Children older than this seem to be able to cope with the conventions of television — the collapsing of time by editing, the conventional language of cutting, the recognition of scale (and change thereof), and so on. They are also likely to be resistant to, and sceptical of, commercials — and perhaps by extension, weak storylines.

At seven and under, there seem to be more gaps in perceptions. The visual language of television is quite complicated and due allowance must be made for this. If you have a strong story, script or format, with good presenters, you do not need tricksy pictures to zjhush[5] up your delivery.

Approaching the script
How then, with so many constraints, can a script be turned into a programme?

Most of the do's and don'ts stay somewhere in the subconscious mind — it just is not possible to sit down and analyse matters in making a programme in the way that a psychologist or critic does to the finished product. If the work becomes too self-conscious, it will also become laboured, self-indulgent or boring — or any combination of these. In practice, the pictures for many scenes define themselves as one works through the script. (This at least gives a starting point.) If this does not happen, if the images do not form, one has to ask what point the author seems to be making, what else is going on in the story outside the dialogue, and then what picture illustrates the point best, and what picture should follow naturally from that. Very rarely, in these circumstances, should one think about what would 'look good', what would be impressive, what would

67

look 'arty'. The result might please me, the camera operator and, perhaps, the designer, but would not necessarily serve the audience best.

With different resources and a different script it would, of course, be possible to take the same subject matter and make a very different product — just as a water colour gives a completely different impression from an oil painting of the same subject: we work to the limitations of our medium, taking advantage of what is available and turning shortfalls to advantage wherever possible. In the series *Happy Families*, for example, we had no possibility of going on location, so we used drawings and CSO (chromakey). We had lots of characters, some with very few lines: we used a small group of actors to play all the parts. The series gained from both these devices which grew out of the need to decide how to make the best use of available resources.

NOTES

1. A very long-running radio programme where guests talk about their lives and reveal their personalities through their choice of music, a book and a luxury.

2. A quote from Martin Riley's script for *Gruey Twoey*, an example of that which is a commonplace for us.

3. *Television is good for your Kids"* by Dr Máire Messenger Davies, published by Hilary Shipman Ltd, page 70.

4. More detail on this subject appears in *Unkindest Cuts? Some effects of picture editing on recall of television news information* by M.M. Davies, C. Berry & B. Clifford, printed in the *Journal of Educational Television,* Vol. 11, No. 2, 1985.

5. A technical term I first heard in connection with costumes, c.f. "a bit of zjhush".

Chapter Six

Working with Children

Grange Hill, 1978

Working with children adds another set of constraints to choices. The obvious one, already examined, is of time. Some children look very good on camera and sound just right, but getting them to hit marks, or use props and speak simultaneously, can be immensely frustrating.[1] You need plenty of patience. Even getting them to say one line with the meaning you feel it should have, or with any meaning at all, can be a struggle. Yet, once cut together, the performance usually gives no inkling of that struggle.

Given these problems, one has to ask how few set-ups can be used to cover a scene, how simple can matters be made to enable the child to do the scene in the minimum of takes. Some children have an enormous capacity for boredom — having to do a scene from half-a-dozen angles, at two or three takes a time, is pretty well guaranteed to prompt the question, "Haven't we done this bit, yet?" (I have even been asked this question in the middle of *rehearsing* a complicated sequence.)

Even if you do not hear this comment, an alternative (and, if anything, more frustrating result) is the child who, from the tone of his voice, sounds as though he is making perfect sense, but who is actually speaking gibberish, because he is no longer listening to what he is saying.

The corresponding danger lies within you yourself. It is all too easy, especially when time is short, to hear what you *expect* to hear. Do listen and watch the action, trust your P.A. (and the sound recordist, if on location) to follow the script. You are more likely to pick up nonsense if you are listening and not reading the script.

Ways round some problems
As you get to know the capabilities of the child actor you can adapt your methods accordingly. It might be expedient, for example, to shoot close-ups of the most easily bored or fatigued children first; to make the most reliable child the one who starts a move, or who has to find the most critical mark. As time goes on, such a child will learn quickly what you want, and your direction can become more detailed and more subtle.

In contradiction to the earlier comment about using the minimum of takes, it is often terribly helpful to have more than one shot or take on any sequence with children, just to give the possibility of doing something about a solecism, or to enable the adjustment of the pace or length of the scene. If a scene is covered with only one shot, you can join or leave late. You can occasionally interject material from another sequence, but, in essence, you are stuck. With even one extra shot, a close-up, a cutaway, there is nearly always more choice. If there is a mistake in the dialogue, you may even have the chance of re-recording, in sound only, the offending section even days later when the particular location or set is no longer available.

Rehearsals: outside/inside
To help a child, particularly one with little or no television experience, it is even more desirable to have pre-location rehearsal than it is for a cast of adults. Even a quick whiz through a dozen scenes on a couple of days, will break the ice between you and the children and will sort out some basic 'business' that works. A surprising amount will be retained, even three weeks later, when the scene comes to be shot.

Clearly, the value of outside rehearsal if you are going to shoot drama scenes in a multi-camera studio is immeasurable. Once again, though, different children will react differently. Many will be consistent with their lines (some have even proved more accurate than the adults with whom they were appearing).

What is less common among children is the ability to show reactions on precise cues, that is to say, precise enough for camera operators and vision mixer. At worst, the child waiting to speak will be mouthing silently the lines of whoever is currently speaking. The intermediate performance comes from the child whose face is a total blank, concentrating on not missing her next cue. In cases like this, it is probably better to set up specific reaction shots and cut a master-take with close-ups (more or less) line by line.

It is very difficult indeed to be sure at an audition into which category any given child will fall. After a while, instinct begins to help.

In spite of all these apparent restrictions, children do have a lot to offer as performers. One area where they can be positively helpful is with the latest 'street-cred' slang. Conversely, if you are working on a period piece, their delivery of archaic dialogue will be helped if they know the meaning of, and the background for, a particular phrase. If they do not understand, the line will sound distinctly hollow!

"Going for a Take"

There are no hard and fast 'rules' about getting the best from children and circumstances alter cases. If a child is under-rehearsed, he probably will not get to the end of a scene without making a more or less serious error. If he is over-rehearsed — perhaps to the point of boredom — then the result may be a flat, unnatural sounding delivery. The boredom will transfer across to the audience. A sense of fun and energy will come across — but only if you let it!

The trick is to catch the right moment and not to have more than a couple or three takes. There is obviously a problem if there are two or more children who require differing amounts of rehearsal on the same scene. The moment to go for a take then depends on the way the particular scene is weighted — who is the more 'important' figure in that particular scene, and for whom is it the more complicated.

I tend to go for a take when I see a good chance of getting something useful on film or tape, rather than wait until I know that everything will work perfectly. This is not the way I would advise shooting a scene with adults. Of course, if a scene is difficult to retake, because your heroes are throwing custard pies at each other, or because something is to be broken, then I would undertake an extra rehearsal or two.

Some children are more erratic than others as performers and can be guaranteed to change something on a take. This is the moment when their concentration level shoots up (you hope). If you know this is the case, there is justification for going for a take earlier rather than later, to show up problems that are not apparent at rehearsal.

SAFETY AND STUNTS

The earlier mention of custard pies leads on to special effects and stunts. A child audience does seem to enjoy watching stunts, and seeing the effect of special effects, electronic and otherwise — although I would hope that the effect would be so subtle that the audience would not be aware what is and what is not 'special'.

Children taking part in programmes are usually, by their nature, more than happy to try anything. No matter how willing they are, no matter how skilled they are (or say they are) at particular tricks, children must not be exposed to danger. If there is any doubt about the safety aspects of a particular sequence, bring in the safety experts and visual effects designers or stunt arrangers. Shoot the scene for safety or get it rewritten! And do consult your company's safety officer.

Most adult actors may be trusted to do certain things, simple falls and the like, which come as part of the actor's stock-in-trade. Child actors may, in the excitement of a take, move

Gruey Twoey. Children enjoy stunts — but not getting wet and cold

73

slightly differently from the rehearsal, may time things differently, may end on a slightly different mark. They may be all right. They may not.

There are many ways of conveying effect. Years ago, I had a boy falling from the top of a multi-storey car park. The main effect was achieved by showing a big close up of the boy's face as he lost his balance and fell (i.e. stepped) out of frame. This was followed by a close-up of his companion, first grinning, then looking horrified, and turning his head as his eyes followed the imagined path of the fall to the ground. The next shot showed the boy on the ground. At no time was it possible for the boy to fall from the car park. It worked. I was subsequently asked by a child, who knew the car park, if we had used wires and a crane. He was convinced he had seen the fall happen.

(This 'cut to reaction shot — cut to result' effect was one I first met on *The Basil Brush Show*.[2] Basil was shown sitting in a dentist's waiting room. The nurse asked him to go into the surgery: the director cut to a close-up of nurse as her eyes followed Basil into the surgery. The next shot showed Basil settling into the dentist's chair. Apparently several people wrote in convinced they had seen Basil walking — something difficult for that design of glove puppet.)

In general, too, safety procedures appropriate to the action ought to be seen to be done. Children and adults should be seen wearing appropriate restraints in cars, should wear protective clothing and padding when skating and skate-boarding, and so on. If these points are not observed, there will be letters to answer — probably from children. It is difficult to prove what influence television actually has, but if a TV hero is shown taking a sensible course of action, it cannot do any harm and might even encourage others to do the same thing.

Matters of fact
If you are shooting children taking part in some hazardous activity that they would be doing anyway, such as canoeing, you must be scrupulous not to add to the hazards. Take the advice of the event supervisors. Make sure your crew is properly fitted out with life-jackets, etc. Do not ask to record or

film an event that the supervisors would not allow were you not present.

Even taking all precautions, things still can go wrong. Your responsibilities are first as a human being, to minimise risks, and secondly, if something does go wrong, to help. 'Getting the shot' comes much further down the list. The test to apply might be to ask yourself if you would happily let a child of your own perform the action for another director.

Under British law, you do also have a personal legal responsibility for safety. Each production team has to have a designated person responsible for safety. That individual must have appropriate basic safety training. If something did go wrong with your shoot, you would not be the first Children's Programmes employee to end up in court.

The BBC demands high standards of safety from all its independent suppliers of programmes and services, as well as its own staff. Familiarity with such rules and proper safety training are essential whoever you work for.

Children being themselves
So far, most of the problems discussed have applied to children as actors. If you are running a documentary, magazine or quiz programme, what then?

Quiz programmes require the selection of children who, like the child actor, are good at being themselves in front of the camera. Sometimes these children may be chosen by the programme maker, and sometimes by an organisation: a school, scout-troop, or the like. The successful ones will probably be the most articulate, confident and, in the context, well-informed of the group.

There are several programmes for children that need more than verbal dexterity — physical co-ordination and stamina may be important for at least some of the rounds. *Eyespy* and *Survival Challenge* fell into this category. *We are the Champions* is an example of a programme where the approach is mainly physical and where winning depends on teamwork. It

75

Grange Hill, 1982

is interesting, because it regularly features the achievements of disabled children, a group under-represented, to date, on television generally.

In documentary and magazine programmes, the children who appear are more likely to be self selecting by virtue of a particular knowledge or skill, or because they have shown bravery or resourcefulness, or have the largest collection of Teenage Mutant Hero impedimenta in the country.

On camera, they may become tongue tied, especially if asked questions off the topic that brought them into that position in the first place. The skill here is in the research. If a child does 'freeze', the interviewer must ask questions that a lawyer would call leading. This should work, but there is a danger that some children will say "Yes" to almost any question posed. The framing of the questions, therefore, must not mislead your audience.

If a commentary has to be added to a sequence, then it is obviously going to be desirable, from time to time, to have the child-subject speaking. This can lead to another problem. You may have a child who can cope with anything or one who is articulate on camera, but who cannot read a voice-over with any degree of conviction. In that case, you may have to decide which is more important, the person speaking in her own words, or the message she is trying to put across. If the latter, you may have to consider dubbing on a professional 'voice'. (There are now quite a number of children with the agencies who have useful experience at voice-over recordings).

Having what it takes
Obviously, in all these cases adaptability and sensitivity on the programme makers' part are necessary. One thing that is likely to put a child off her stroke, is the awareness of a sense of frustration on the part of the director.

This is not to say that you must never show irritation. Children can play around, procrastinate, and be difficult. At times, a sharpness in your approach (or in that of the production manager, on a drama) is useful in refocussing the minds of the children taking part, especially if proceedings have been hampered by technical delay, or by the weather.

In general, however, whatever the type of programme, the children are there because they want to be. They will possibly be missing school, they will usually be enjoying seeing how programmes are made, and they will have almost as much interest as you in getting things right. The nature of children's programmes, too, is that the child is likely to be at the centre of attention. All this works to your advantage.

Problems can begin when a child does not have enough to keep him busy — boredom can set in, and disruption, whether through bad behaviour or lack of attention when it is time to act, can be a problem. This crops up when there are many children on a shoot, or where they are peripheral to the main action — as in some 'adult' dramas. Plan for expenditure of excess energy — some form of physical activity is necessary for all children, and your production may not supply the scope for this without consideration on your part.

If the child is central to an adult production, as in an adult's evocation of childhood, then this problem would not arise, but there might be others. In *The Evacuees*, by Jack Rosenthal, the story concerned two Jewish children billeted with a gentile family during the Second World War. The children were made to eat pork, and were understandably revolted. The two Jewish boys playing the scene were given sausages to eat which they were told contained pork, but that special dispensation had been given by the rabbi. Nonetheless, the two child actors showed a very real revulsion when the scene came to be shot. Afterwards, they were told that the meat was not pork, after all. The director had just wanted an intense reaction from the boys. He got it.[3] Is this kind of subterfuge justifiable? Does the end justify the means? I think it is highly questionable.

NOTES

1. There are further remarks on this topic in *Continuity Notes* by Roger Singleton-Turner published by BBC Television Training.

2. Basil Brush, a fox, first appeared on ITV in 1962 working in close association with Ivan Owen.

3. The story is told in full by Maureen Lipman in her book, *How was it for you?*

Chapter Seven

Finding Children

'Wooly' (Danny Collier) in *Gruey Twoey*

There are many people who are disparaging about the full-time stage schools in the U.K. They will tell you that the children at such schools are precocious and mannered, incapable, therefore, of giving a natural performance. There are children like that, of course, and there are children (however likeable) of no discernible talent at such schools. Some, however, can be very good as actors.

These schools are also likely to be able to provide you with children with special skills, such as tap and ballet dancing. They may not be of an exceptionally high standard, but the children are likely to be better than those in a similar sized group from an ordinary school.

If you need high-quality dancing, then there are stage schools where the emphasis is on the musical skills, rather than acting. There are, too, many dancing schools up and down the country, mostly full of little girls, who dream of being ballerinas. As an after school activity they can be a great deal of fun, but they could also be a source of talent for your show.

Aprés l'école
There are similar 'after school' or Saturday morning groups that specialise in drama.

Such schools can now be found in many parts of the country. Some are primarily for educational purposes and are not set up for a director's convenience, although they are, usually, only too pleased to see some fruits of their success on television. Others perform a similar function, but have an emphasis on their agency aspect.

If you are wanting children for small parts, or as extras, this should be fairly easy to arrange. You do not need to have a particularly exclusive approach in the selection. If, however, you are hanging the success of an entire series on the performance of one child, or even on the performances of a small group, then you may need to see large numbers in order to find the right ones. If you have a family of six to cast, as I had in The Story of the Treasure Seekers, this is a major, time-consuming, operation. Finding children who speak with Stand-

Happy Families (Mr and Mrs Hay the Horse)

ard Received Pronunciation, who may sound right, therefore, as middle-class Edwardians/Victorians is harder, these days, than to find good actors with regional accents.

On that production, the children not only had to act well and sound right, but also had to appear credible as a family. If in doubt, always go for the acting ability — family likeness can be imagined, good acting cannot. Years later, on *Happy Families*, we did not bother about family likeness at all, the casts were ethnically integrated and this did not detract from the popularity of the series.

In the 1950's, it was illegal for young children to act on television at all, so perhaps some productions from that period suffered from children who were rather long in the tooth! There are advantages in working with more mature children, but credibility suffers. The problems change.

It is true, incidentally, that adults watching children's television sometimes have difficulty following heavy regional accents, and they often write and complain. Children seem to have less of a problem with understanding and very rarely complain in this way.

If you are looking for a child with a particular regional accent, then you will probably find that there are not enough stage schools or acting classes in your target area, other than London, to give a wide enough choice. What then?

Local education

There is a very useful book[1] — revised annually — which lists all the local Education Authorities, all the State run, and State affiliated secondary schools, and all the State middle schools in the country with names, addresses and telephone numbers of the Authorities and head-teachers.

I have always found Local Authorities very helpful — and they usually will be, provided they know what is going on![2] There is often a drama adviser listed. If there is not, there will be an English adviser in each authority. They can tell you which schools in your target area have the strongest drama departments — they might even make an initial contact for you with individual schools. If they do not, you can at least claim some official backing when you contact the head-teachers, or the heads of Drama or English, at the individual schools.

There are currently a number of schools that have 'opted out' of their local Education Authorities. As with public and other private[3] schools, it is perfectly normal to make contact directly.

Bear in mind that the Local Authority can grant or withhold licences for children and are also entitled to send inspectors to studios and film locations in their areas. They have the power to send children off the set, even if this means stopping production. Quite apart from considerations of good manners and legality, therefore, it is prudent to follow the proper procedures. In my experience, the advisers have on the whole been very positive and have saved me a lot of time both with their schools and in liaising with the Educational Welfare Officer, or whoever oversees the granting of licences.

Most schools are happy to let their pupils take part in children's programmes, provided proper provision is made for education, and provided your project will not interfere with GCSE's too much. (In selecting children, this is a major factor.) On the whole drama teachers will offer you their best pupils in the age range and sex you specify. They will weed out the ones who they think will not cope or whose academic life is unlikely to survive a brush with a television company. They will probably have a few front runners, who have done well in the context of their own school productions. These star pupils are not always the ones to fulfil your requirements, but they are rarely less than interesting.

There is a big difference between primary and secondary school children, even where there is only one year's difference in age. The primary children, in my experience, are less aware about drama and the demands that are likely to be made. That is the advantage of either type of stage school for this age group — the children are likely to have seen scripts and will have done some improvisation (even if they do not always recognise the word).

If you need pre-school children, there are more difficulties. There are few guarantees with children of this age about anything they may be required to do. Long dialogue sequences are likely to be impossible. Some agencies can help in providing children who have always been around studios and who will not therefore be fazed by the lights and the fuss. Then there are the children of staff and, if you are feeling sufficiently foolhardy, your own children.

Auditions
There are many different approaches to auditions, and what you ask of each group of children, and each individual, will be governed by what they would ultimately need to do in your project. You may have to see many children, so whatever method you choose is likely to be one that does not involve too many repetitions of a basic explanation. You will need time to allow yourself to gain a decent impression of each child and time for the child to feel that she has had a fair chance. You will need to be aware that children are not necessarily good

83

sight readers and that this may be the first time they have actually met anyone from the world of television.

In trying to bear these things in mind, I have evolved two basic approaches:

At a stage school, whether full or part-time, I tend to see the children in groups of about six — this is especially true if there is a group of that number to cast, who all have one or more scenes together. I briefly explain who I am and what the project is, then go round the children noting names, ages, birthdays, and some feature of appearance, that will help me link the right face to the right name, later.

The next step is to get each child to tell me what appearances he or she has made recently, emphasising speaking parts. If there is nothing, then any subject, like how long they have been coming to the school, will get them talking — you will hear their natural voices and begin to get an idea of their characters. Ask about any special skills needed at this stage, too, e.g. dancing, roller-skating or bike-riding. Most children will be very honest and quite revealing on such subjects, even in company.

The next step is to split them into groups to prepare an improvisation on a topic of your choice, or one they have done recently themselves. I find three to each group is a good number. Pairs will take too long, any number over four will mean someone will not get a chance — they will be swamped. Also, more than three will be confusing as you make notes. If a child is cut out of an improvisation or has been swamped by the others in the group, this may in itself indicate that the child is not as outgoing as, perhaps, he needs to be. If I want to check, I run a two-handed improvisation myself. I might be the heavy parent, for instance, demanding where the poor unfortunate has been until this time. This is also a useful exercise if you have an odd number of children or you feel a child has been let down by a lack of capacity in his colleagues.

One tip: I always *tell* the children to concentrate on each other, and to ignore me. I then move around so I get a good view of their faces. If their eyes follow me, if they are grinning in an inappropriate way, or if they are otherwise not concentrating, it will show up at this point. If their eyes do follow me, it is quite likely that the camera will distract them, too — and nothing destroys the illusion of television so much as an unrehearsed look into the lens! Obviously, if you want a child to talk to camera this may not matter, but I still think it is an indicator of a lack of concentration.

What else do you look for? Inventiveness, an intelligent approach, a thought-out storyline, a clear idea of the character being portrayed are all important. Then there is the extra ingredient, possibly the *quelque chose* that indicates a sense of humour, consistent, believable facial reactions, the little feeling in the pit of the stomach that identifies the child who can really act.

At this point, it may be appropriate to read a scene. It is useful to choose a scene where there is an adult that I can read, too. There is a lot to be learnt from the way a child reacts to your reading — sometimes with a look, sometimes with a clarity of thought, and sometimes just with a sense of timing. You will find that there are children who are dyslexic, and there are those who can barely read even at thirteen. Some of these may still be able to act well and, if there are not too many lines to be learnt, they may do very well indeed. In current BBC productions the scripts are important and featured children do have a lot to learn. Good reading skills are important.

Obviously, you should not expect brilliant interpretation at this first reading, but a fluency and some feeling for language are necessary. You may well find that the interpretation of certain lines becomes an 'acid test': if the child reads the particular line with understanding, then he or she is worthy of further consideration. An inability to find a proper meaning on first reading is not, in itself, sufficient reason to reject a candidate. However well or ill a child gives a first reading of a speech, it is always worth getting him to repeat it with a different emphasis, trying to convey a different meaning. As a last resort, you can try getting the child to mimic your own intonation.

What all this indicates is how well the child is likely to interpret you and your directions. Do not be impressed by credits as long as your arm in other productions — particularly in the theatre — what ultimately matters is how well you can get this child to work with you.

If you visit a non-stage school, you are quite likely to be presented with a room full of all the children you are to see. This is easier for the school than the disruption caused by removing groups from class on and off through the afternoon. You may have a drama teacher with you for all or part of the time, too, who is likely to have put her most promising pupils before you, but there may be the odd ones who are there simply because "it will do them good to meet someone from the BBC". The school is putting itself out for you, so this is a small price to pay.

These children will not be used to auditions, but they will probably be used to improvisations. After the introductions, I begin by 'breaking the ice', opening a discussion about television programmes in general and children's programmes in particular. It can be interesting and you may learn something about how your most cherished views on the subject may not mean very much when explained to a class of children.

Once this is over, I then move on to improvisations, possibly as arranged by the teacher. At this stage, after all, you need to see what the children can do in the most favourable circumstances.

At the end of all this you will have page upon page of notes, and a list of children you want to see again, especially if you are casting major parts. Once you have cut this list down to manageable proportions, which means a short list long enough for you, and short enough for the producer, you can move on to round two.

A well-known producer/director of children's drama once said to me that you usually 'know' when you have the right child for a particular part. I have thought I have known — and been wrong; and have thought a child was right for one part — but cast him in another. I have also had that gut feeling that I was going to cast a particular child almost from the beginning. If there are not two or three children on the short-list who, I feel sure, could cope with each part, then I probably have not seen enough children. These front runners may be overtaken by a dark horse. In the long term, this does not matter. Selecting the best child does. This is more important than personal feeling. There have been times when I really wanted a particular child to get a part and ultimately I have had to cast another. It can be tough saying "No", especially after round two.

Round two

So far, all the children, with the possible exception of the one or two suggested by adult agencies,[4] will have been seen on their home ground surrounded, more or less, by friends, certainly by a peer group. These circumstances are more favourable than those under which you — or they — will be working.

The next step, therefore, is to arrange a meeting on *your* home ground for the front-runners. You might choose three children for each part, maybe more, maybe less. This meeting will probably involve your executive producer, producer, or equivalent. (Of course, you may find that the selection up to this point has been made by a casting director. I have never had the luxury of such services and would probably miss the chance to get out and about and talk to this diverse selection of our audience.) Once again, we see the children in groups, preferably in some way relating to how they might be cast, e.g. in sets of potential brothers and sisters.

It is likely that some of your favourites will not produce the goods on strange territory. You can try the best children from each group in combination with the best of other groups. Ideally, numbers of children and your time should be arranged so that the first in can read with the last in, if necessary.

Trying different juxtapositions like this can be very interesting, and children can shift from one character to another, before your eyes. On one series, *Gruey*, I had in mind several possible combinations for the part of the hero, Gruey, and his best mate, Wooly. In the event, Wooly was played by Danny Collier, whom

Gruey Twoey

I had marked as a possible Gruey. Kieran O'Brien played Gruey. I do not think any of us regretted those casting decisions. Kieran, though, had been in my mind as a possible villain. Despite standing out at the audition as one of the best child actors I had come across, he did not then tie in with my mental image of Gruey nor with the author's scripted description.

The moral here is that you should always go for the best available acting ability and, if necessary — or appropriate — adjust the physical description in the script or the original book. This was not an option for another part in the first series of Gruey. One of the main characters was called Quidsia Rahim. This is a Muslim name and, in 1987, in Greater Manchester, it was difficult to find very many girls (or even boys) as extras from such a background whose parents were willing to let them take part.

When we came to plan the second series, the girl concerned chose to pursue her school career, so we took the stories in a new direction, notwithstanding the fact that she had come over very well on the screen.

Sometimes, if you have seen a large group of potential actors, you end up needing a third day of auditions to make final decisions, and to give enough time to try all the combinations. This may seem hard on the children, but there is nothing to be gained by casting children who are not up to the pressures of performance. They will not thank you and neither will your backers — a six-part drama costs a lot of money.

Parents
As the short-lists are arranged, it is important to let the parents know in some detail what is going on, which project the auditions are for and the commitment of time you would be expecting from their offspring if they were selected.

Parents may not be aware that their children get paid for television appearances and that the law governs how this money is banked on the child's behalf. They may not know that, by the same law, tuition has to be given during term time (q.v.), that chaperones can be provided and that hotel accommodation is paid for separately. A covering letter with the details of the later auditions can answer most of these questions before they are asked. This helps to avoid your being placed in the position of casting a child and then finding that the parents will not let him take part.

The other thing to remember is that some parents will have booked their holidays well before the start of auditions. This can be a problem and should be sorted out before your short-list is finalised. Parents, however, are often very accommodating and, sometimes, for a minor part, it is relatively easy for you to juggle the odd day or two.

Parents who send their children to a full-time stage school are generally more knowledgeable in such matters than those who do not, although this is not always the case.

Chaperones and tutors
Sometimes, parents or grandparents chaperone their own family. This can work, but chaperones are needed for all children on the unit, even if they only appear for a day, and it saves money to have one licensed, experienced, chaperone

89

looking after up to twelve children, rather than having numerous family members on or around the set.

Chaperones (once known as matrons) are people deemed suitable to look after children employed in films, theatre and television. They must have a licence from their own Education Authority and are paid for by the programme. Parents and grandparents do not need a licence. Other relatives, even sisters, do. The minimum age for a chaperone is eighteen (at the time of writing) and more men are doing the job now than used to be the case.

Properly speaking, each chaperone is responsible for a specific child or children, and her[5] name will appear on that child's licence. A good chaperone is extremely valuable. She will make sure that a child is on the set at the appropriate time and that he is delivered home safely afterwards. She will look after the child during the day and, if you are on location, during the night, acting *in loco parentis*. She also has a duty to stop you overworking a child and exceeding permitted hours.

If there are more than about three children and if the budget permits, I find it helpful to have two chaperones (notwithstanding the legal limit of twelve children per chaperone). This is especially useful if you have children of each sex. If there is a problem, it is easy for one chaperone to cover for another should a child need to be taken elsewhere for any reason.

You may also have to hire a tutor. The better tutors get in touch with the schools attended by the younger members of your cast, find out about their particular syllabus and teach appropriately. Obviously little in the way of scientific experiments can be covered, but one tutor, working with the appropriate text books, can achieve a lot as he will be working with only a small number of children.

By law, the children must aggregate an average of fifteen hours of tuition per week, averaged over a two week period. This tuition must be of one type, i.e. with the appointed tutor, or at the child's school. In practice, this school/tuition mix can be a little more flexible than the words imply.

It is possible for a properly qualified tutor to register as a chaperone and to combine the duties. This only works with a limited number of children, since the probability of being able to release all the children at the same time for tuition is remote and there should be a chaperone with any child on the set.

Once more, individual circumstances alter cases. There is a degree of variation in the way Local Authorities interpret the rules. If there are areas of doubt, or circumstances not covered exactly by the book, it is always worth someone from your production team talking to the relevant Educational Welfare Officers (or the equivalent). Obviously, the first concern is for the physical and mental well-being of the child and the second is for academic progress. If there is then a way, within the rules, to ease the production process, it could well be in everybody's interest for the Authority to allow a concession.

Why bother?
The business of employing children is quite costly and time-consuming all round. It is not fair — or legal — to expect children to battle on in the face of 'flu, chicken-pox, or, indeed stomach ache. Adults may be expected to know when it is safe and right for them to carry on (except when they are being 'noble' and a potential hazard to themselves and, perhaps, others). With children, you cannot take any chances.

In addition, children can be very erratic in their performances, which is also time-consuming — but it is part of your job to iron this out, to keep up the quality both by good direction and by careful editing.

But why bother with children, why not cast small 16-year olds? It is true that a 16-year old can play younger: with the late onset of puberty (and an unbroken voice, if male), possibly as young as 12. If you have only one child, this may work. If you juxtapose real 12-year olds with your 16-year old, it will show up — the difference in maturity, mental, rather than physical, will tell. You can get away with it on stage, but not usually on camera. It is also worth bearing in mind that your falsetto 16-year old may suddenly shoot up and become a baritone in the course of a long production. This can certainly happen in the

91

span of a year, which makes a follow-up series less desirable and reduces the chances of sales. The 1950's productions that were allowed only to use teenagers now sound remarkably husky.

An exception to this was the BBC production of *Tom's Midnight Garden*. Here, the director cast a 12-year old boy as Tom, playing opposite a girl who had to age from 12 to 18. She was convincingly played by Caroline Waldron, then aged 18. The factors that helped were that for much of the story she was supposed to be older than he; she always wore Victorian dress; she was a girl — covering the same age range with one boy would be much harder. The same character also had a brief appearance as a 5-year old. In that sequence she was, of course, played by another girl of the appropriate age.

NOTES

1. *The Education Authorities Directory* published by The School Government Publishing Company Ltd.

2. In other words, do not make initial contact directly with schools run by local authorities. The schools may check back with head office about 'these television people' and somebody may take umbrage.

3. In the U.K. this makes perfect sense. 'Public' schools are private, but not all private schools can be called public. Schools that would be called public elsewhere in the world are often called State schools.

4. These may be no better than the average you have already seen — but there will be some children from this source who are well worth seeing.

5. Most chaperones are women. I feel easier in having a woman looking after girls, than I do a man, unless he is the father of one of those concerned. It has never been a problem in my experience having a woman looking after boys (although there are stories I have heard about very young chaperones and a certain lack of discipline). If you are not actually working away from base, any potential problems are reduced. The proportion of men among tutors is much higher than it is among chaperones.

Chapter Eight

Caution, Child at Work!

The Borrowers

Whatever type of programme you are making, there are aspects of it that may be novel to the children with whom you are working. They may have considerable experience on stage or in commercials, but the latter will not have given them any experience of sustaining a character, and the former is not a good preparation for working on location.

Whatever their track record, the children may have reached your production without anyone having explained why they have to hit marks or why, for example, they always have to pick up a book in the same hand. Perhaps no one has explained about 'checking the gate', or what a hair is, or why an aeroplane — even a distant one — can cause a retake. It is surprising (or perhaps not) how much more patient a child can become if these things are explained, if he can see the reason for all the hanging around.

These explanations need not take much time and you do not have to do them all.

Public places
If you are shooting on location, the probability is that you will spend some time in public places, parks, shopping precincts, streets and so on. Obviously, all the usual rules about safety apply and all the problems of noise and so on will crop up. An additional hazard arises from the fact that word gets around that you are making a programme for children — especially if it is a second or subsequent series. This news may attract an element of nuisance, which may vary from a handful of children offering help and peering over your shoulder (or under your elbow, perhaps) at whatever you are doing, to a group of older youths who may find it amusing to throw things at the unit. The shouting of obscenities during a take also seems to be a popular sport. Your unit is, from the crowd's point of view, trespassing on their home territory.

Whatever the position, and even if the crowd is merely friendly and curious, it is a good idea to keep them away from any children on the unit you may have. Polite firmness rules! If your child performers are allowed too much mixing, squabbles based on the on-lookers' jealousy can break out, your performer may find difficulty in coping with autograph hunters, or ribald comment about the series, or television in general. This is what the chaperones are there to prevent — their responsibility is the well-being of the child. Trying to be nice to a group of total strangers can also simply be too tiring for the child-actor.

Of course, if there is time, and especially if you are in the neighbourhood for any length of time, it is probably a good idea to allow a carefully supervised 'autograph' session. Mostly, children will respond well to this and to a generally friendly approach by the unit.

Obviously, you will not be in a public place without the police knowing of your presence and you will need to employ a policeman or two if your work involves disturbing the normal flow of traffic. (Again, there are safety regulations on this topic.) The size of the problem varies very much from one area to another.

Tuition
The difference between filming on location with children and adults probably shows up most in tuition. This is often arranged on board the unit coach and so problems will arise if several cigarette-puffing, chatty extras also wish to rest their weary bones there, or when it rains, and the whole unit wish to shelter.

Rain is not the only difficulty. The coach often becomes un-bearably hot in the sun. Ideally, you set up a classroom in a near-by church hall, or in a quiet room in a house that is not being used as a location, unless that house is very large. This may involve extra expense, but it is not necessarily too great if combined with some other location facility, such as lava-tories. It also helps children concentrate and gives schoolwork a more effective standing in the schedule. It obviously puts the tutor in a stronger position in dealing with the more unruly children, too.

Remember that periods of less than 30 minutes do not count to the overall average of 3 hours per day! This means you have to be able to gauge pretty accurately how long it will take to get a child to tuition and back, and ready to restart, perhaps after a costume change. Prompt decisions need to be made, with accurate assessments as to how long, say, the next lighting set up is likely to take. You may have to resign yourself to the unit twiddling its thumbs for a while, for a lesson to be completed. This is when a stand-in may be useful in giving out-of-vision lines or in testing lighting and so on. A double (in the right costume) may also help for over the shoulder shots, for instance. This means more expense, but it may be justifiable if there is a particularly heavy load for one child.

Remember, an inspector can turn up at any moment. If the records are not up to date and correct, he can remove any child from the shoot.

The tuition, as explained earlier,[1] is a legal requirement. If you are working in term time it must be provided. Remember, no matter what the children have to say about it, the dates of the term are those, not of the child's school, but of the local authority where the rehearsal or performance is taking place. Tuition has its limitations, but it can make the difference between a child reaching expected examination grades and failure. I know that formal education is disturbed in these circumstances and I would not want to be responsible for possibly spoiling a child's academic career, and subsequent life, for the sake of 150 minutes of television. (Children's drama operates for the most part in 6 x 25 minute episodes.)

There is another side to this, of course, especially for the child who will appear only in one or two series, and then return to 'normal' life. For brief periods spread over a year or so, that child will be working hard with adults in a new environment. She will learn about the process of making videos or films and will mix with people of wide experience. She will be earning money, will be treated as a responsible person, and if she rises to the occasion (most do), her opinion will be treated seriously and on a par with that of the adults around her. This ought to be beneficial and to help broaden her horizons.

There are times, too, when a child who has certain areas of difficulty at school may be able to catch up, given a personal

96

tutor. After all, most children do not get anything like 3 hours of their teacher's attention during a normal school day.

Wrapping up well!

In my experience, children on location tend to be either stoics or whingers.

Even a moderate breeze can prove to be chilling on what might seem like a warm day to a director. Performers have a lot of hanging around to do. Children grow cold quicker than those continually in motion — and quicker than they may realise themselves.[2] The chaperones or the Costume department, should make sure that children are well wrapped up between takes, during lighting adjustments, script conferences and in breaks for tea. It is a good idea to give them something warm that is incongruous — an adult sized anorak, for instance. This will not be left on inadvertently as a take starts.[3]

Gruey. The author directing on location — in the summer, 1987

Most children will not ask for such consideration, they will not complain because it is not 'done' to appear weak, or because they have not realised that they are cold. There are those, though, who like to make their presence felt every time you see them by complaining of being too hot, too cold, too wet, or too thirsty. It is interesting that this category is rarely the one into which the busiest children fall.

It is because a child may be covering up pain or discomfort, too, out of loyalty to the programme, that you should play safe and call in medical advice earlier rather than later, or send a child home (provided there is someone there to look after him) and lose one day's filming if he seems ill, rather than risk losing the whole project because he has contracted double pneumonia.

There are sound business reasons for this, of course, but this should not be the first consideration. We have a duty of responsibility as producers and, more importantly, as people.

For these reasons be extremely careful about anything that might be hazardous. Children are often willing to try things, to take risks. They must not be allowed to do so — except in the context of interpretation. Even entering water, running or stagnant, 'fresh' or salt, is now regarded as a possible hazard. This is largely because of the increase in the number of rats in the country, which possibly can spread Weil's disease, and because many of our beaches are polluted.

NOTES

1. See pp. 54, 90, 102-3.

2. The scientific basis for this concerns the ratio of their mass to their surface area: a mouse loses heat more rapidly than an elephant.

3. I do not know who had the idea in the first place, but I am indebted to the BBC Costume Designer John Hearne for this piece of wisdom.

Chapter Nine

In the Studio

Hartbeat

So far, most of my comments have applied to children working on location. Working in the studio is a somewhat different matter.

There are many advantages to studio work, especially in a multi-camera set-up. You are, for a start, working in a controlled environment. It is not going to rain, unless you bring in visual effects staff; aircraft noise is not going to be a problem; you will not have to deal with hordes of passers-by; you will not be troubled by traffic, and you have the full back-up of the studio's capabilities — canteen facilities, dressing rooms, make-up and wardrobe areas, technical expertise and, in varying degrees, property and design facilities — each according to your budget.

The advantages for children are that there should be no difficulty in finding a proper room for tuition; that it should be possible to shoot a rehearsed sequence in one or two takes, in a single pass — i.e. without having to repeat a scene for close-ups or reverses; that the whole process is likely to be warmer and more comfortable than a location.

If a shoot is complicated by video effects, and progress is, like film, shot by shot and slow, it is at least still faster than it would be on location.

If a sequence is of any complexity, it is desirable, if not essential, to have a period of outside rehearsal. This provides time for experimentation, for trying out different ways of approaching the sequence and to learn a consistent set of moves and words; time to work out shots and technical problems, and ways round them; and time to get to know your cast, adult and child, and for them to get to know each other[1].

The fact remains that most children I know prefer location work, as it *seems* quicker and they find it more exciting than the studio, unless they become fascinated by the technical process, or unless there is a fully practical Space Invaders machine as part of the set. (At least in these circumstances you know where your junior cast, and half the camera crew, will be during meal and tea breaks!)

Children's hours, again

The rules and regulations concerning children and studios are slightly different from those governing locations. It is in practice possible to have children of 12-plus in the studio for up to 12 hours for 1 day in the week, up to 10 hours for 2 days, or for up to 8 hours for 3 days a week. In most cases there are two caveats:

- The child must not work at all for the rest of that week.

- The child can still only work the permitted three (if 12 years old), or three-and-a-half hours a day (if 13 or over) within those hours.

The regulations stipulate 13 as the age for these concessions, but they also state that, in these respects, a 12-year old may be considered as a 13-year old.

By contrast, it is permissible for a child of the appropriate age to be on location for up to 8 hours a day for 5 days a week. I suppose there is perceived to be less pressure on location, as there is less ground to be covered each day. When *Grange Hill* first moved its studios to BBC Elstree, it was decided to work in blocks which included 2 weeks with 3 consecutive days in the studio. The 3-day/8-hour restriction applied. A special case was pleaded and, as a concession, the cast were allowed to be present for a technical run for 2 hours on the Monday morning. If children's interests are safeguarded, this is the sort of special concession that may sometimes be permitted, given plenty of warning, by local Education Authorities.

In one of my productions I also needed some children to perform in the studio on 3 consecutive 8-hour days. In this case, there seemed to be no objection to our rehearsing for 2 days in that week and recording on the other 3. The children were, however, not working more than 4 weeks within the overall 12-week production period.

The rules are open to interpretation: the interpretation, and the rules, are amended from time to time. *Make sure that you know your local current practice!*

The best use of time?

So far as outside rehearsal hours are concerned, there are several possibilities. Your production may allow working all day, and releasing small numbers of children for half-an-hour at a time for tuition. This only works if each child is in a relatively small number of scenes. Even if it is possible, it does not mean that it is a good idea because the children are continually having to adapt to something different and time is lost at the beginning of each time-segment. Tuition is the aspect that suffers more, though. Instead, you could call the children at 9 a.m. and release them in time to get 3 hours tuition either at their own school or from the tutor, or call them at about 1.30 p.m. *after* they have had 3 hours and lunch, at their own school, or with their tutor. In the first case you have them when they are at their freshest. In the second, they probably get more actual schooling, you have them until 5 p.m. and they still have time for the proper breaks.

It is the latter system that I prefer. If there are any 'adults only' scenes, these can be rehearsed in the mornings, part of which is also usually free for planning, updating running orders and camera scripts and so on.

Of course, if the children live, or go to school, more than a half-hour's drive away, then it will almost certainly be necessary to arrange for tuition, just as you would on location. This is a major consideration on a series like *Grange Hill*. There are several rooms set aside as classrooms at Elstree Centre and the tutors are in regular touch with the schools of all the child actors.

It is highly organised — as indeed it needs to be. The children are collected from their own schools and brought to Elstree for outside rehearsal, where they work until 4.30 or 5 p.m. In the recording weeks they are brought to the studios from pick-up points near their own homes and, after changing into their costumes, are taken to the location, the studio or to their classroom. It is expected that children will not be asked to travel for an excessive time each day. If any individual child does live far from your studios or place of rehearsal, you may need to arrange hotel accommodation for the child to stay with the chaperone.

Tiredness

Of course, a schedule that includes a lot of tuition and many shooting days is very tiring for any child. This is the reason why the number of performance days is strictly limited to 80 for 13 to 16-year olds, and to 40 or 20 for those under 13. This is the reason, too, why much of the BBC's children's drama shooting takes place in the summer, over the school holidays. On a series like *Grange Hill*, which has an almost all the year-round schedule, there are many children, so the weight on any individual is lessened.

On the shorter series, it is quite common for the whole project to stand or fall by the performance of one or two children. The strain on them is therefore proportionately greater. Anything the production can do, like scheduling itself across the summer holidays, is going to ease matters and make for a better result. (The drawback to this is that your production may delay or shorten the holidays of the child-actor's family. Most families do not mind, once in a while, but a regular disturbance to one child in a family can become a problem.)

Tiredness — day by day

The inspector usually appears only once or twice in an entire production, if at all. The chaperones are also frequently very sympathetic towards the production. Most children will try their best to do anything you ask of them. Why not, therefore, ignore the rules and just go on shooting till midnight?

There are several reasons. One is that someone is going to have to fill in a time sheet, sign their names to it and send it to the Local Authority. The Authority will halt production or the form will lie. Another is that there will probably be quite a large overtime bill, except for the children, who technically cannot be seen to do overtime. The main reason, though, is that you will end up with a very tired child who will not be able to give of its best, neither after the scheduled hours, nor the next day. The work will become drudgery, the performance will begin to lack life.

Abusing the system is counter-productive. In any case, the main consideration should be for the child. In the worst case I know a child star suffered a nervous breakdown and has never recovered her former position. (Her work was not, primarily, for a producer of children's programmes.)

Even when all the rules were being followed, I have seen a 12-year old's performance fall off at about 4 p.m., even though tuition had finished with the end of term and the rules were being followed. It would have been cruel, in those circumstances, to have insisted on dragging things out to the last permissible minute of the allotted time. All you can do is to be prepared for this to happen and to try and keep the most complicated shots for the earlier part of the day. (I know it is not always possible to do this, but if you aim in the right direction, you can hit the target most of the time.)

At the chaperone's discretion, it is possible to go over the allotted time, occasionally, by half-an-hour. If the children are still fairly fresh, this may save you, and them, from awkwardness over rescheduling or a return to a difficult location.

Children are rarely as articulate as the adults with whom they have to work. They have not the life-experience to pace their energies out for a day, much less for a week or for the months that a shoot can take.[2] It is therefore unrealistic to expect the consistency of performance in unfavourable circumstances that you buy when you book an experienced adult actor.

These comments of special consideration can apply, too, to those not technically children, but not yet fully mature, the 16 to 18-year olds. Again, be aware that EC regulations affecting the employment of this age group are liable in the future to affect film, television and theatre production, as well as other walks of life.

A good child actor is usually capable of delivering the goods with no apparent effort and will be treated on more or less equal terms by the whole unit. In other words, there are levels at which you may forget you are dealing with a child. I worked with a boy of 14 as able and versatile as some actors 10 years his senior. I have, too, employed a girl and boy who, at 10, were able to sight read a script with all the assurance of a good

14-year old. Yet they were both at primary school (or equivalent) and were still very much children.

When is a brat not a brat?

There is another side to all this care and consideration, of course. A leading child will be the centre of attention, an Important Person. This does sometimes go to his head, so it is important to make sure that discipline is maintained and that the child does not start throwing his weight around with people like dressers and make-up assistants, who may need the director's back-up in restoring a proper sense of order. One major part of the director's job is to decide when a child is under stress and when he is just being difficult or seeking attention.

Communication

Getting a performance from all the people on the unit is as much a part of the director's job as interpreting the script. How the individual does this will vary with the individual. For all that I am frequently accused of looking worried, I like a light atmosphere on my shows and, insofar as I achieve this, I do not analyse how I do it. "If it ain't broke, don't fix it." You will need to work out your own approach.

One thing to remember is that all children are different and will bring different experiences to their work. You therefore need to develop specific methods of communication with each one.

In terms of actually giving directions, I try to keep as a last resort the "Say it like this" routine. I am not trained as an actor, therefore I may not be saying a line in quite the way that I intend. A bad example can be destructive. Discussing what the line actually means can help, especially in the sense of reminding the child of the context — of what happened in the last scene, notwithstanding the fact that you do not shoot that until next Thursday. Asking for the emphasis to be on a particular word can often be surprisingly helpful, too, in clarifying meaning for the child as well as for the audience.

If a child says a line so that it makes sense, but not the sense (or the whole sense) that you expect, you may be fighting a losing battle trying to get the precise inflection you want. You may also find that there are more, valid, ways of saying the line than you expected — and that you should accept what is on offer with good grace. The losing battle will waste time and may undermine the child's (or your) confidence, thus proving destructive. You might also have been wrong in the first place!

If there is a problem check that the script is correct. Would a contraction, "does not" to "doesn't", for instance, be helpful? Would an interjected, "Now," or "Then," help the rhythm? Is there an archaic word in the way? ('Groovy' is a good example in today's scripts). Was the line correctly typed in the first place? Talk to the writer before rehearsal begins and see what his attitude is to minor changes of this nature — or use the talents of your script editor, if you have one. A badly delivered or incomprehensible (because uncomprehended) line helps no-one, least of all the author.

If there are problems injecting a particular emotional intensity into the line, try and get the child to go right over the top. Sometimes you may have to demonstrate what you mean by over the top. Do so, even if it makes you look silly — it may help your child actor to become less inhibited. Sometimes comment from other children or adult actors can improve matters and reference to the most intense moments in the child's life may also help.

There will be times when you run into a brick wall. I once asked a 12-year old to show me he was frightened, having just confronted what he thinks is a real-life burglar in the dining-room. He could not convince me. I tried everything — all the recommended tactics. There was a problem — he claimed never to have been frightened! We ended up having to work out what he might do in similar circumstances. His throat might go dry and he would swallow. His voice might become a little unsteady, and so on. It was no good doing anything like leaping back in amazement, because it just looked false and was wrong in the context. The scene was all right in the end, not good, just all right.

Of course, the problem could, in this case, have been with the director.

Dealing with groups

If, as is frequently the case, you have to deal with a group of children, what then?

Individual strengths and weaknesses become apparent: the time you can expect one child to maintain interest in a scene, the range of facial reactions during another's speech, readiness to react, accuracy of timing, reliability with props and so on, are all factors to consider when the time to shoot arrives. For instance, it may be expedient to govern how you shoot a scene, especially on one camera, according to the length of time each child may be expected to concentrate.

In a multi-camera studio, the way you script reaction shots will depend very much on the reliability you can place in a child giving those reactions at a fixed place in the script or, at the other extreme, how likely the child is to be mouthing the 'incoming' lines, or looking at the camera, or any other distracting object. Of course, you can shoot a lot of specific cutaway reaction shots, even on a multi-camera production. This is fine, but it eats into both studio and editing time. The more that can reliably be shot in 'real time', the better.

It is a nice feeling when it all works.

A tip or two

There are two things I have observed regarding dialogue: one is that there are many children who find it difficult to say scripted interjections like "Oh", "Eh", and "Ah" no matter how much they normally use them. So often these little words sound false to me. They are better cut, at least at the learning stage, and, if you are lucky, re-inserted just before the take.

The second is the broken sentence. This can sound very wrong. The boy who is to be interrupted will invariably stop short, exactly as scripted, but before the girl (who is interrupting) picks up her cue. If the implied next words are not clear to you, ask the writer what was intended and add the next word or two to the rehearsal script. Then get the 'boy' to say them. Get the 'girl' to interrupt at the original point and everything should come together. There seem to be few writers who insert

107

these extra words in the first place. In a purely literary context, of course, they are not necessary and may not even be heard.

If you have a choice, it is sometimes helpful — especially in a single camera shoot — not to begin at the beginning. The first scene that the audience sees should look good and be assured. The first scene to be shot may well lack this assurance. At this stage, everyone is still getting to know each other and, in the case of a child, his capabilities and limitations. For the same reasons, try not to begin with the final scene as this, too, needs a firmness of touch which may be lacking at the start of the shoot.

It is also probably worth avoiding 'first scenes' and first meetings when auditioning for major parts. Hearing the same scene dozens of times may distort your view of it, and may allow the 'auditionees' to clutter their minds with unwanted preconceptions — one of them will get the part and the last thing you want is a mind cluttered with preconceptions!

All this is the fine detail, but it is the fine detail that can, if blurred, mar any director's work.

NOTES

1. There have been many changes in the past decade in the way actors are booked. Individual deals are now commonplace, including 'buy-outs' of residual rights. There has been pressure from some quarters to go for a daily rate. There seems to be a danger here that rehearsal may be discouraged. Yet, as already indicated, much time can be saved if interpretations, 'emotional paths', moves and 'business' are worked out before shooting begins. There are complexities in booking adults as well as children!

2. Sometimes the children do not help themselves by going off at lunchtime and working themselves into a lather over a game of football. This can damage costumes, as they rarely think to change first. It can also cause problems to the make-up artists, if the children become very flushed for an hour or two after the game. This is apart from any considerations of fatigue as the afternoon progresses. On the other hand, it can be a necessary release of pent-up energy.

Chapter Ten

Tactics and Truth

Watt on Earth in Titipu

Much of television is about illusion. This is true even of magazine and documentary programmes. Their illusion is that they show the viewer reality, life as it really happened. What is actually shown is a selection of events to give an image of the reality (or, indeed, of the truth) as perceived by the scriptwriter, the director or the picture editor.

Suppose you are shooting a record of real events as they happen to a child: a demonstration of skills; the preparation for a concert; a comment on the trials and tribulations of permanent physical disability, or whatever. You and your camera may witness a reaction to failure, to losing the 'final', to an admission of the awfulness of life. These reactions are not, or should not be, caused by the production crew, nor should they be for the crew's benefit.

If an emotional outburst happens and the camera records it, then it may be legitimate to show it,[1] even at the price of your child audience being distressed in sympathy. Each individual case needs to be judged on its merits, but the ultimate question might be: "Does this sequence really help our particular audience to a greater understanding of the world, or is it merely a piece of kitsch tele-journalism?"

Emotion in drama
What all successful drama gives us is a picture of some truth about the human condition, therefore of some sense of reality. This is as true of a Miracle Play, a Noh performance, even of something as apparently unreal as an opera, as it is of a brilliant reconstruction in a docu-drama. There are many film makers who want to get every last detail authentic, who always want to work on location, because "everything must be real". It seems to me that they may become bogged down in a hunt for the reality of the image. This can become time-wasting, and can detract from the truth the film maker is trying to convey — especially if it is accompanied by mumbled lines and heavy duty actuality sound effects.

The whole point of drama, I suggest, is *illusion.* You do not need to distress a child actor to portray a distressed child. If

The Borrowers illusion illustrated

the script calls on a child to cry, talk about crying at the audition
stage, see what the child can do there.

I once worked with an actress of twenty who was required to
cry. She performed the scene most movingly, but was unable
to stop herself from crying until a minute or two after the scene
ended. She was so convincing, I did wonder for a moment or
two whether she was genuinely distressed.

In comparison, I worked once with a brilliantly instinctive 12-
year old, who could not bring tears to order. She asked for a
piece of onion, to help. She did not cry — but she looked
sufficiently close to it, physiologically, for the scene to work as
well as the one described in the previous paragraph.[2]

Most children who are likely to be selected to act these days
will have some experience of improvisation. Many of the
improvisations will have involved explorations of aggression
and other strong emotions. You should, before you cast,

explore such areas in improvisation and script-reading with the likely candidates. If you do not, you may be disappointed when the vital scenes crop up.

Always remember, though, that there are several ways in which individuals cope with emotion, therefore there are several convincing approaches. If a child cannot find one way, he may find another. (If the worst comes to the worst, a blank stare, appropriate music and good reaction from the nearest adult actor might get you out of trouble.)

Anger and aggression seem to be emotions most children find they can portray. They can also often cope well with grief. Tenderness, especially between boy and girl, can be more difficult, and comedy — or a sense of fun and irony, combined with good timing — can be much harder to find.

If one child in a group has to show deep emotion, you will probably find that the others are helpful and constructive. However, one or other of the less sensitive ones may utter a disparaging comment at an inopportune time during rehearsal, embarrassing the one with the problem. Such things do happen occasionally and you must deal with them. Asking the sarcastic one for his approach can be helpful — either through the constructive comments elicited or by shutting him up.

Sometimes, if there is a problem, moving on and then returning to the problem area can be helpful. If you do this, ensure that you leave enough time to recreate the mood of the scene you postpone. It is no good deciding that a scene is difficult and then putting yourself in the position of having to rush it.

It is reasonable, therefore, to allow plenty of scope for a child actor at emotional moments. You may not end up with what you planned — but you may get something stronger by showing flexibility than by insisting on one particular form of expression. Excessive pursuit of 'real' tears — the reality of the image — may backfire.

Beware, too, of artificial tears — glycerine can be too transparent a device.

Playing it cool

Frustration at a child's lack of ability may build alarmingly, but there are almost no occasions when a director's loss of temper with the child is likely to help. The most common reaction is for inhibitions to result for a time because of the ensuing embarrassment.

If the show of temper is directed at a child who is failing to deliver the goods, then that child is just going to feel confused about the scene. If the child is merely misbehaving, or not concentrating, then he is likely to become more unco-operative, at least in the short term.

In these circumstances, I find that a lightly delivered threat to cut down on the individual's close-ups can be efficacious. As a last resort, I point out that they are the ones who will look foolish on the screen, as the audience never sees me. This usually does the trick.

Chronicles of Narnia

If anyone is going to be the 'heavy', if there has been a real problem of extreme thoughtlessness, it appears to help if it is the production manager or the chaperone who is seen to be furious. The children then turn to the 'cool' director in some relief.

Principal children are usually pretty co-operative: they have plenty to do, they want to look good, they like to be thought of as 'professional'. Disruption is more likely among those with small and non-speaking parts. I have only once in a quarter century of television, seen a child sent off the set forever (for petty vandalism around Television Centre), and this certainly had a salutary effect on the rest of the cast — even the less co-operative principals. In this case it was the executive producer who took the decision and, of course, the responsibility.

If a child becomes difficult, it can be useful to know what is going on at home. If there are matrimonial and other parental difficulties, it will temper your approach to a child having an off-day. This is not to suggest seeking deliberate involvement — in all probability you are only going to be in that child's life for a few weeks. The whole point of your relationship is that it is professional, and with the child, not with the parents — the work may well represent a haven for the child. (This is an incidental reason for avoiding some parents as chaperones.)

Once a series is over, there is a degree of 'after-care' due from the production, if requested. This can mean warning a child that he may be in for some unfavourable reactions from his school fellows, or it may amount to answering questions about career matters, insofar as you are competent to do that. It might even mean helping with a request for work experience. I always try to discourage my 'charges' from taking up acting, however good they are. If I succeed, it means they probably would not, as they do not have enough dedication. If they succeed in spite of this discouragement, and in spite of having worked on one of my series, I am pleased.

Bitchiness
Obviously, due allowance has to be made for age and capabilities in all your dealings with the child-cast. This works in

many ways. I once heard two boys, on their first day working together, discussing their previous experience. One recounted a list of television appearances, including a couple of Shakespeare plays, which sounded quite impressive. Then he said, "What have you done?" As it happened, the second boy had also had his moments in a few plays at the National Theatre. Both boys were aged eleven.

I have also had scenes between very experienced boys and a couple of girls, somewhat younger, who had never done any television at all. The more assured boys were very critical over the deficiencies of the girls, their lapses of concentration, and so on. It really did become necessary to point out that the boys made mistakes too and, if they made fewer, it was perhaps precisely because they did have more experience. It has been my experience that, in a group of the same age, it has usually been the girls who have been quicker to respond and who have concentrated longer and harder.

Communication
In your dealings with children, allow them to have their say — they know what it feels like to be a child *today*, and you do not (as my daughter frequently points out). Allow them to enjoy the process of making television programmes — even if (perhaps especially if) the material is deeply moving. If there are problems, let them know what is going on — delays are boring, but it does help if you know why you are waiting. Also, a child who knows why you are asking him to do something is more likely to do it properly — or to be able to suggest an improvement of his own. (see *Going for a take* on p.72).

The crew
It is important when assembling your crew and adult cast to make sure that everyone knows the approximate ages of the children concerned, and that the show features children heavily, if this is the case. Some actors may not like this, and there are some crews who will not be too keen, either. It is always helpful, if you have a choice, to find people who are in sympathy with your material and your audience.

If all is working well, the children will like, and be liked by, the other performers and the crew. Much is likely to be new to the children and they may take an intelligent interest in how the machinery works. So long as this interest turns off when there is work to be done, and so long as there is no danger, it should be encouraged — they will learn something new about television, the crew are usually happy that their work is appreciated, and everything makes for a good atmosphere. The children might actually become easier to work with, especially on technical matters.

"Don't forget the diver!"

Adult actors' needs must not be forgotten in the concentration on, and nurturing of, the children's performances. As the director, you are the first audience of the actors. Their job is to expose to millions, via television, emotions usually displayed only to their nearest and dearest. It takes an unusual kind of person to do that well and they will need your encouragement, attention and direction just as much as the children. In fact, if the children have been chosen, because they are good at being themselves in front of the camera, whilst saying other people's lines, they may need less real work than the adults. Many children will not understand the term 'motivation', still less will they need it explained. I have seen children unable to find a level of emotion, but I have not seen one show any *Angst* about it in the way that some adults do.

A trained adult actor may well use a range of 'techniques' — not to simulate an emotion, but to enter into what is happening in any given situation — there is still a lot of control and dispassionate observation needed to act even in highly emotional scenes.

So far as choosing adult actors is concerned, they need the security to let a child be 'centre stage', to be the hero or heroine. An adult who needs constant reassurance, who needs to feel at the centre of things himself, is likely to feel the full strength of the old adage, "Never work with children and animals". Fortunately, such individuals are rarer than some of the stories might suggest.

Shooting out of order
All filming, and most studio productions, other than 'live' shows, are likely to be shot out of order.

With a set of long scripts to hold in their heads, children are likely to become confused. In practice, those I have worked with, mostly nine and over, do not. They rely on you to tell them what you want. They will play each scene as it comes and will need to be reminded that their pet goldfish died on the previous page, or that they are about to receive their long expected birthday present in the next scene.

Adults will have far more idea of where they have come from, and where they are going, in these terms. They are consequently the ones who will want the discussion as to whether they are on the right track. It is actually easy to lose the place yourself, unless you do your homework! The story order is most useful as an *aide-memoire*[3].

Planning
It is vital that you get the most out of the time and resources allocated to you. For this, you and your team, need to plan very carefully. What fixed points are there (i.e. is there anything that can only be done on one or more specific days)?

Next, work out the way to get the most from the children. If there are any night shoots, for instance, can they be scheduled on a Friday, so that the weekend can count as the children's two compulsory days off afterwards? There are more rules associated with the Licence, on this topic, too. It does save many problems if you can manage to shoot 'day for night'.

If you put difficult scenes early in the day, then difficult matters don't have to be rushed and lighter scenes can, if necessary, be simplified if time runs away from you. Work out if there are ways of getting more gaps for tuition time into the schedule.

Remember to avoid starting a schedule with a very difficult scene, or the first scene of the series — everybody is still getting to know each other. Performances will grow and relax as time passes.

Do not forget all the other criteria of saving money by booking people for the shortest possible time, allowing the best system for travelling (if applicable) and for contractual and union agreements about the length of the shooting day, engineers' meal breaks and so on — and on.

It really is a tricky business and it repays time spent on it. It is also worth noting that the production manager will schedule primarily for economy, which is not necessarily the best thing for the children's performance. Check the P.M.s work!

Ultimately, the schedule should allow the children in your cast to make the most of their limited time. If there are things that can be sorted out at the post-production stage, go for that. Shooting time is more expensive than editing!

NOTES

1. I exclude the sort of intrusion on personal grief that is so distasteful on adult television.

2. See also *Don't forget the diver* on p.116.

3. Your P.A. should be able to produce one. There are further details in *Continuity Notes* by Roger Singleton-Turner published by BBC Television Training.

Chapter Eleven

Selection of Shots

The Borrowers

Having finalised the script and booked the cast, pictures are the next priority. Let us leave aside the ever-changing technology and assume that you are shooting in the medium most appropriate to your project, with the most appropriate crew. The real question to answer is this: what pictures will best tell your story?

There is, of course, no general answer to this, but there are some key factors to consider:

- What is likely to be the best location for each sequence?

- Can this be an actual place, or can it be evoked well in the studio?

- What combination of shots of your presenters or actors will best inform the audience of the progress of the story, be it journalistic or dramatic?

- When do the words in the script say all that is necessary, and when would the script be best augmented by a change in the picture?

- Do your actors or presenters look right, are they in the right clothes, have they the right variety of clothes to help distinguish changes of time and season, for instance?

- Is their make-up right?

- Are all the shots composed and lit in the best possible way?

- Are there enough pictures to give a pleasing (but not too restless) variety and pace?

- Is the continuity correct?

- Have you given sufficient consideration to sound?

- Have the sound recordist's problems been considered, discussed and overcome?

- Have you selected the best source of music? (Have you allowed for the fact that children do not have to be fed a constant diet of 'Pop'?)

- Have you enough time and facilities to edit and create any necessary effects and to dub?

If you can satisfactorily answer all these questions, then you should have something that will cut together well, a production that should be polished. To these should be added, most importantly, a caring for, and a commitment to, the programme idea, for this will inspire the rest of the team. On top of all this, there is that extra element that we all seek, that results in a quality programme. (If this could be defined and quantified, then there would surely be more high-quality television available across the world.)

It follows that if there is a deficiency in any of these areas, the programme will suffer as a result.

Undoubtedly, the skill and the experience of the director will help to make up for any shortcoming in the budget, or for a lack of facilities and time, etc. This can, though, only be taken to a certain point before the quality does suffer.

Several times, I have been in the position of having time to shoot a scene in only one way, that is by making it work in a single shot. This pre-supposes that each actor will perform equally well on the same take. When some or all of the actors involved are children, this is by no means a foregone conclusion.

It is often desirable to design scenes to be shot from two or more angles to allow for editing, and the removal of unwanted pauses, and to tidy up an inexperienced performance (not to mention to let you edit the programme for time and pace!).

If a scene will best be done as a single developing shot, that is great — but you should not be forced into the position of making sequences like that on account of lack of resources. There are enough compromises to be made as it is — the

121

weather, for instance! Resources — and their cost — are these days the determining factor in television production.

I would dislike strongly being forced into the position of having to shoot a drama with personal microphones (which do not, at present, give the best sound recording quality) because the production accountant has said that the production could not afford to have an assistant sound recordist to hold a boom.[1] Similarly, it is a great limitation to be refused lights, merely because you are working out of doors (that is in a high ambient light-level). You will be in trouble very quickly at the editing in matching shots, unless you have had a day (or sequence of days) of *constant* light cloud, or *constant* sun.

There is also a very strong argument, even when money is tight, for the presence of a production assistant to keep proper continuity notes.[2] Even when shooting on videotape, much time and discussion can be saved and re-shooting for continuity becomes virtually unnecessary. There are many occasions when a factual programme goes on location without a P.A., and there have been some low-budget drama shoots also without anyone trained in taking continuity notes. It is hard to see how this really makes a unit more efficient.

Money is important and strict budgetary control has become increasingly necessary in television, so it is still sensible to take a project and cost it, and do it at that cost. If you do not have the resources, you have two options. One is to try and find a way (by writing-out, perhaps, the burning houses or the crowd scene that can only be effective with many extras), or of otherwise making the project fit the budget. The other option is to abandon that project and to do something that is inherently cheaper.

At least if you take either of these courses, the end product will be properly finished in all respects. However, given the time-slots a network planner has to fill, there is a danger in the latter approach that only cheap and easy projects will be attempted. There will be a tendency to do nothing that cannot be done in modern dress, or nothing that cannot be shot within a-half-hour's drive of base, or always to avoid a large cast.

To date it has been possible to dramatise stories with settings in many parts of the country. This has allowed us to involve children from many parts of the country, with the variety of accent and background that this gives. In order to do this, we spend money on travel — naturally. In the future, the key question is whether money will be available, or whether cost-cutting exercises will reduce the scale, scope and quality of programmes for children.

IMPORTED PROGRAMMES

One way to save money is to buy in programmes that someone else has made. If you really want to save money, then you can show programme-length commercials about *My Little Pony, Care Bears* or *Sylvanians*, or one of several more series that are aimed at making the world's children want to buy a particular range of products.

Of course, these films do not always create the expected market demand, but for one brought up in public service broadcasting, it is difficult to accept that the primary motive for making any programme should be to sell something, rather than to entertain or inform.[3]

There are many animations available which are both entertaining and attractive, especially those from Eastern Europe.

There are imported live action dramas, but these are now mostly made for a family, rather than a specifically child audience. Given our continued insularity over languages, most of these need to be dubbed into English, which can work well, especially if the series has been shot with dubbing in mind (i.e. not too many close-ups, and not too many long expositions). Sub-titling as a solution to the language problem probably makes life too difficult for too many of our young audience. An alternative to the fully characterised dub, and also to sub-titles, is to have an explanatory commentary read by a single voice.

There do not seem to be very many documentary or informational programmes from overseas for children. Perhaps so far too few have been suitable for adaptation into English. In the future there may be scope for the sort of international co-operation for children that we already see on series for adults such as *Horizon* and *Wildlife on One*. There has already been one such project, on museums, and there are hopes for something to follow this up.

CABLE, SATELLITE, AND ALL THAT JAZZ

Much has been talked about the access of independent producers to our terrestrial transmission system. New independent production companies are seemingly springing up (and going bust) every day. Many of these supply material to the satellite and cable companies. At one stage it was said that the average cost allocated for children's programmes was £5,000 per hour. This was not a lot. Since then, BSB and Sky have merged. If the new company (and any later rivals) prove successful, it may be that they may find more money to originate programmes!

There is a problem for television in general in the expansion we are seeing, because real talent and creativity are likely to be spread more thinly. It seems probable that money is also likely to be less available. Both these factors would suggest that there could be an overall fall in quality, both technically and artistically — and this will affect children's programming along with all others.

NOTES

1. Sometimes it is necessary to use personal microphones to harvest the sound — for instance, when working with puppeteers.

2. For a fuller explanation of the significance of continuity, see *Continuity Notes* by Roger Singleton-Turner, published by BBC Television Training.

3. You may think this a natural reaction for one working in the BBC, yet the BBC was the first to show both *Thundercats* and *Teenage Mutant Hero Turtles* in the U.K.

Chapter Twelve

Puppets

Mortimer and Arabel

Of course, one way to avoid employing children is to use puppets instead. I tried that on *Happy Families* — all children under ten, all dogs, cats, parrots, horses and even the extras were puppets or cardboard cut-outs. They were appearing with people in sets that were heavily stylised, and I think the combination worked. The small 'children' in each case were required to act and react in a way and at a length that would have been difficult to sustain using conventional children. The animals all had very specific things to do and would almost have been too real in the context of this particular series. We felt sufficiently confident about the concept after the first series to continue the convention into the second. This idea seemed to be acceptable to the audience.

Many other programmes have mixed puppets with humans, from *Muffin the Mule* and *Sooty* onwards. *Sesame Street* and *The Muppets* have been extremely imaginative in their use of this mix. Basil Brush usually appeared with at least one human, so did Mr Turnip and so, of course, do all ventriloquists' characters. *Dizzy Heights* was another BBC programme with an off the wall (or Heap and Wall)[1] humour.

On ITV *Grotbags* used amazingly sophisticated dialogue, and a variety of unlikely characters in the company of the eponymous heroine, a green-faced human witch.

All puppet series fall into two main groups:

- Animation, such as *Postman Pat, Wind in the Willows* and all the many others.

- 'Real time' puppetry, such as *Andy Pandy, The Flowerpot Men, Toytown* on the BBC, and *Four Feather Falls* and later, *Thunderbirds* on ITV.

After the early days, 'pure' puppet programmes in this second category became much rarer on the screen. There is likely to be a resurgence in the middle of this decade, as there is a pool of television/puppet talent and an expertise in shooting of puppets that has grown up in the wake of work by the Henson Organisation both here and in the U.S.

The United Kingdom has a long tradition of puppet entertainments, most obviously with the Punch and Judy shows that used to be found in every seaside town. The Little Angel Theatre in London has an honourable history particularly with marionettes.

Further afield, marionettes were considered worthy to entertain royalty in Austria among other European countries. They have been established for centuries as adult entertainment in Sicily, and were not beneath the notice of Cervantes' itinerant and self-deluding knight, Don Quixote, in Spain. Whole villages looked to puppets for entertainment in India and the shadow puppets of Java reached a high degree of development. In Japan, the hand puppet has been developed to as high a degree of sophistication and beauty as you can go without electronics.

The significant thing about many of these examples is that they are no more 'for children' than the puppets of *Spitting Image*[2]. On television there has been relatively little puppet activity for adults, apart from *Spitting Image*. There was a series many years ago called *A Small World*, which, if memory serves, used marionettes. Gillie Robic made a series based on *The Decameron* for Channel 4 with shadow puppets. This was for adults, but followed in the tradition I remember from my childhood of the shadow plays of Hans and Lotte Reiniger.

This list shows that puppets are not inherently and solely for children. If it shows anything else conclusively, it is that the word 'puppets' embraces a whole world of entertainments. There is little in common between, say, the enormously successful re-run of *Thunderbirds*, and the still popular Sooty, or the work of the Henson Organisation. The popular puppets have clear characters, are clearly not human, and in some respect have to do with exaggerations of reality. Some projects need humans, some need animation (cartoons) and some need puppets. All need a good script and a good format.

Incidentally, puppets are not necessarily a cheap option. It took up to five operators beside Francis Wright to operate the Psammead in *Five Children and It* and its sequel. In *Mortimer*

Mortimer and Arabel — the sets

Mortimer and Arabel — in the workshops

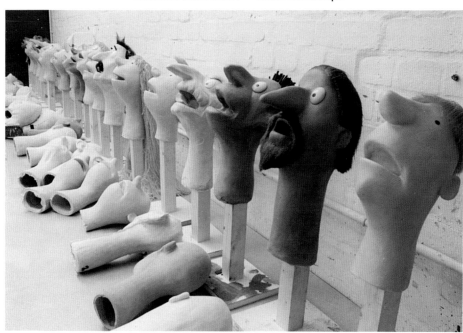

and Arabel it has been necessary to build all the half-sized scenery and make or adapt each and every prop. This work, carried out by a BBC Visual Effects design team led by Malcolm James has been a massive undertaking. To do all this properly, it cannot be done cheaply!

There are special techniques to shooting puppets favourably, but perhaps the most important are these:

- It can be difficult to arrange a puppet in such a way that it looks at its best from more than one angle at once.

- Rod and hand puppets are generally operated from below, so high angle shots (seeing feet and floor) may present problems.

- As a puppet is inhuman — that may be its strength — lingering close-ups on long dialogues or speeches have their limitations.

- The puppeteer is producing a whole-creature performance with his hands. It may often be better, therefore, to set the camera further back in order to see as much of the action as possible. The whole puppet body is expressive and the close-up limits what you can see,

- Two or more puppets together in a shot can work together well, acting and reacting.

- Puppets may be incredibly complicated with many degrees of movement and many operators. There were, for instance over ninety puppeteers operating the monster plant in the film version of *Little Shop of Horrors*. Puppets can also be very simple, like Sooty. In *all* cases, the most important single secret of maintaining credibility is 'focus'. This means that the puppet must appear to know where it is looking at all times. This element of performance is even more important than lip-sync.

- Many puppets have mobile mouths. These are usually operated by the hand of the principal puppeteer. A good

On the set of *Mortimer and Arabel*

puppeteer will maintain a surprisingly high degree of mouth synchronisation.[3] It is not as easy, therefore, to record lines as wild tracks and sync them up later, as sound recordists may lead you to believe.

- The best results with puppets are achieved if the puppeteer speaks the lines for his character as he is operating the puppet. This means, of course, that pre-recording dialogue is not deemed to be a good idea, at least by good puppeteers. Pre-recording limits what a puppeteer can do and leaves no scope for 'business'. If necessary you can post-sync dialogue, either with the puppeteer or with another voice, should your puppeteer run out of voices.

- Puppetry is physically very hard work and rehearsal, other than in terms of character and voice development and script-learning, is impossible until you put the puppets themselves on the set and in front of the camera, for it is only at this point that the puppeteers can see the frame in which they have to perform.

Mortimer and Arabel — the author directs 'over the garden wall'

- As puppets are not human they can be exploited in the same sense that cartoon animations can be — both can behave in literally fantastic ways.

- Although floors are difficult, much can be suggested. There is a lovely sequence in one of *The Muppet Shows* of Kermit the Frog tap dancing. In spite of the fact that his feet are heard, not seen, it is very funny, and quite convincing.

If you have not worked with puppets before, talk to the puppeteer about what his needs are, so that working space is used sensibly. Look at the possibility of raising the sets and the camera so that the puppeteers can stand upright to work. Discuss with your sound recordist where the puppeteers' microphones will be (e.g. on headbands or on specially made armatures, close to the mouth). Check how many monitors are needed and whether your puppeteers need reverse scan so that a leftwards arm movement produces a leftward image movement (think about it!) The ideal is to have switchable monitors, so that the picture can be shown in a normal mode for puppets who have their backs to the camera. (Some puppeteers, e.g. in the Henson Organisation, insist on using only normal scans). On *Mortimer and Arabel* we usually had six puppeteers (with additions when we had six or more characters needed at once). Each principal required a separate monitor. Sometimes all six monitors were needed even when only two characters were visible. This was most likely to happen if one or more characters had to 'walk' for a distance.

If you are mixing real people with puppets and raised sets are impossible, then plan carefully where your puppeteers will be hidden. Allow for trolleys for them to move around. I have used two types, one is a low box-stool on wheels about a foot square and the other is a flat board with a back support at one end, on castors, so the puppeteer can slide easily across the floor, keeping her head below the bottom of frame.

On television, there are obvious problems with stringed puppets — it is almost impossible to conceal the strings and the movements are notoriously less crisp than those for hand and rod puppets. They have their place, though, and in the hands of experts can be very entertaining.

Puppets are (usually) exaggerations of humanity and so their reactions and their whole reality can also be exaggerated. To get the best out of them be bold.[4]

Animation

This is the area of a specialist. Animation is expensive to make, but relatively easy to dub. There are many short cuts, too. The animation in a new American series will be much simpler than in a traditional Disney film. All the great Disney movies showed subtle animation of the whole figure and those figures usually had shadows. More recent animations have relatively few moving parts and are often shadowless. They are, therefore, simpler and cheaper to make.

There has been a small but healthy animation industry in the U.K., of course, for many years. The BBC has commissioned dozens of animations, like *Postman Pat* or *Rhubarb*, to name only two of very different styles. ITV companies have commissioned many animations too, and Central Television and Thames have both supported their own very successful animation subsidiaries, Filmfair and Cosgrove Hall Productions respectively. Animation is not a soft option for drama: at several hundred pounds per second, you need to be very sure of your market before you embark on such a major investment as Cosgrove Hall's *Wind in the Willows*.

NOTES

1. Heap and Wall were the human stars of these series.

2. *Spitting Image*, the development of Fluck and Law, has been a long-running and biting satirical series, using life-size latex caricature hand puppets.

3. I have seen this done with two puppeteers operating two puppets, with one of them performing the lines for both puppets. This is an impressive degree of teamwork.

4. These comments need to be treated with caution where puppets are mixed with live action humans, and where the puppets are used to produce actions of imaginary, deceased or difficult creatures, e.g. the dragon in *The Chronicles of Narnia*, the dinosaurs of *Jurassic Park* or the sharks in *Jaws*.

Chapter Thirteen

Viewers' Reactions

Blue Peter, 1986

There is much that can be learnt from analysis of viewers attitudes towards programmes. You can tell which age groups, which sex, which social group, which area tuned in to your programme in the greatest numbers. You can see from one week to the next how figures change — as a show builds a loyal following, or as the delights of out-door play, and what-ever is the latest fad on other channels take their toll.

It is interesting to compare the numbers of children in the audience for top-rated adult programmes with those pro-grammes made for children. For some age groups, it would appear that the Australian soap, *Neighbours*, has for some time been the most popular series among children. When this series is on, however, there are no broadcast children's pro-grammes in competition. Many adults like the series too, and perhaps watch with their children. Its rival, *Home and Away*, has also built itself a loyal following.

The most popular programmes, even then, do not get more than about 40% of all children watching them. That means 60%, at least, will be doing something else! With both BBC and ITV showing programmes for children at the same time, it is considered that if more than 17% of all the children in the target age group watch (bearing in mind that there are not usually figures for the under-fours), the series is very successful, regardless of how many adults are watching too. Although it is all too easy to become embroiled in a numbers game, there are some interesting things to be learnt from the audience figures: they cannot be ignored. One statistic to remember is that only about 30% of homes in the UK actually have resident children — 70% do not. These households may well complain about the protected children's sector if licence money is spent on programmes that are palpably failing to reach the publicly-stated audience.

MATTERS OF PUBLIC CONCERN

Language and accent
Many matters concern or upset television viewers. The point has been made that adults, on the whole, write to the television

companies to complain, while children write to participate, or to praise (or to ask for autographs, which can legitimately be taken as praise, I think).

One of the main grounds for complaint is whatever is perceived as 'bad language'. There is an argument for cutting all expletives and another for reflecting a greater realism. Drawing the line is a matter of fine judgement.

There is a need from time to time for a word of emphasis to help a speech rhythm, or to depict honest emotion, and there can be a problem finding something suitable, and something that does not sound weak. Each case needs its own solution.

Another aspect of language is tone. Many of the complaints in the case of *Grange Hill* concern the cheeky or violent tone in which a line is delivered. I think the justification — if there is to be one — must come from the context. I suspect, too, that some complaints come from parents and other adults who do not like to think that schools have changed so much since they were young.

There are complaints, too, about accents. It generally seems to be the stronger urban accents that provoke the greatest reaction. Note, again, that this reaction is from adults. Also note that we take a lot of trouble finding children who will come across well — and this nearly always means they use their natural speaking voice. We hardly ever ask a child to 'put on' a special accent. In fact, it is more likely that we will spend considerable effort trying to achieve greater clarity. (Incidentally, any lack of clarity in a child's speech seems to be exacerbated by the use of current models of personal microphones.)

The basis of the complaint is that we are encouraging children to depart from 'proper' English. This seems to be somewhat unfair: if we used only 'middle-class' accents then we would be rightly accused of being 'exclusive'. The focus of the problem is the 'bad grammar' that seems to come with some accents. When do bad grammar and a lazy accent become dialect? Maybe the answer is to keep the dialogue in the best

137

grammatical order you can, so long as it sounds natural in the mouth of your particular cast.

Sex and difficult subjects

The treatment of sex in children's programmes is another area likely to provoke quick and angry reactions. Our audience has a curiosity about sex, but I am not sure that it is our place always to satisfy that curiosity. I would try to avoid the misleading and, if appropriate, I would encourage caution — even monogamy.

In 1993 *Jackanory* took Raymond Briggs' story, *The Man*, and, using a combination of the original and a few specially commissioned illustrations, followed the text closely, as usual. The story is told in dialogue form and none of the actors appeared in vision. At one point, the Man, who is only a few inches tall, is shown urinating. This liquid flow was animated for the television version (a first in children's programmes, I believe!) Within the same month, an adaptation of Morris Gleitzman's book *Two Weeks with the Queen* was also shown for older children. The story concerns a boy, Colin and his reactions to being shipped off to the England while his brother is treated for cancer. In the course of all this, he meets a homosexual man (part of the reference in the title), whose partner dies of AIDS during the story.

I had a number of reservations about this book, based on the number of 'issues' you can usefully include in a relatively short adaptation like this, and the suitability of some of this material for an audience that would certainly include some young children watching without an adult to fill in and explain difficult concepts, such as homophobia, homosexuality and sibling death. It is a fact that both *The Man* and *Two Weeks with the Queen* brought in a larger postal response than is usual. The bulk of the former were complaining about the urination. The bulk of the latter — in a ratio of around ten to one — were in praise of the sensitive handling of difficult topics.

The handling of teenage pregnancy on *Grange Hill* has been interesting. Obviously some schoolgirls have babies. It could only be a matter of time before a pregnancy was written into

Grange Hill. (It took about a dozen years — I remember discussions on bringing this subject into an early series, but there were other storylines felt to be more appropriate at the time.) In the event, the tone was very practical, emphasising how much of a tie it is for a student to have a baby. The character decided not to have an abortion and marriage was felt to be out of the question. Moralising was largely avoided and there was no sense of judgement, which would perhaps have been out of place.

Such subjects are difficult and need to be handled with care. It is not part of my job to 'promote' any sort of '-ism'. We in television may put forward the latest theories and facts. Any of these may be open to reinterpretation at any time. However, it is not our function to be dogmatic, or deliberately to counter or replace parental authority, or to denigrate the deeply held beliefs of viewers, parents or children.[1]

Violence

Many letters complain about violence on television — although few on this topic complain specifically about children's pro-grammes. Violence, actual or implied is, of course, a major concern as to its effect on children. Some teachers have said that little boys became noticeably more violent in their play after the advent of a programme like *The A-Team*. This is not conclusive, though precisely the same complaint was current during the run of the Fifties radio series *Dick Barton — Special Agent*.

The dangers fall into two parts, the first is that individual children may be upset, the second is that they may be encour-aged to react in a violent way themselves. The *BBC Producer Guidelines* are clear on the subject and are supported by other reference works).[2]

Two quotes from the BBC *Guidelines for Production Staff* of 1987 may be helpful:

● "There is much confusing and inconclusive research into violence on television and in society. While it may not be possible to establish the nature of any relationship, it is prudent to assume that there may be one."

- "PROGRAMMES FOR CHILDREN
  There is evidence that violence in circumstances resembling real life is more upsetting than violence in a fantasy setting. The distress felt by some adults when violence occurs in a familiar setting or between familiar figures is likely to be increased in the case of children. Violence in situations (for instance, in the home between characters resembling their parents), or towards characters (for example, pets), with which the child can sympathise should, therefore, be avoided. Although it is morally satisfying, especially to children, to witness the success of good over evil, the means employed by 'good' characters should be carefully chosen to avoid confusion with the 'bad' characters. The dangers of imitation are particularly real among children, from whom it is important not to conceal the consequences of real-life violence. for example, a blow to the head must not, in a realistic setting, be seen as a trivial matter without serious consequences."

Since these words were written, new guidelines were introduced with similar effect in 1993 and research from the U.S. has, it seems, established a causal link between television violence and violent acts.

Advertisements (and violence)
Some adult viewers are very concerned about advertising and particularly about the amount of advertising on commercial stations between and within children's programmes. Children do recognise advertisements as separate from programme material from quite an early age. They do not seem to recognise quite so quickly that the advertisement is there to stimulate the child into demanding something he may or may not want, by putting pressure on the parent.

Although children may be moved to respond in a purchasing way to advertisements, in a constructive way to series like *Hartbeat* and *Blue Peter*, it does not follow that they will necessarily respond with negative actions to extortion rackets shown on *Grange Hill*, or to violence shown on *The A-Team*, and its ilk. Dr. Máire Messenger Davies has some interesting comments on this subject:

> "It should not be too difficult to spot the fallacy in this argument. If you are somebody who needs to buy break-fast food for your family ... you will be able to see the difference between somebody persuading you to buy cornflakes (which you need to do anyway) ... and somebody persuading you to kill, maim and destroy, which is almost certainly something that you don't particularly want to do. Thus, in the one case, the advertisement is suggesting to you a course of action that you are quite happy to follow anyway, whereas in the other case *The A-Team* is suggesting (if, indeed, it is suggesting — de-picting and persuading are not synonymous) a course of action which you are unlikely to follow in your wildest dreams."[3]

There remains the possibility that a child will, out of perver-seness, copy that which is shown to be anti-social, or dan-gerous. This is why we take great care in how we show knives, guns, and the like. We avoid showing children handling a gun, wherever possible.[4] Where not possible, great care and thought goes into what we do show.

You do need to be very careful. It is so easy to show something that is regarded by some proportion of the adult audience as undesirable. I once received a letter of complaint after showing a magician drinking a magic potion from a green octagonal bottle. This shape and colour is, of course, reserved for poi-sons. The fact that the magician was instantly transported to another location was, it was suggested, almost an invitation for children to drink from green octagonal bottles. This was my fault although, in my defence, octagonal green bottles *are* much rarer than they once were.

There is always the possibility of children playing games based on what they see on television, and some games may lead to a child damaging him or herself. We have no choice but to take care.

One of the most obvious areas to watch is the treatment of the meeting between a child and a stranger — especially a male. Fantasy or magic and a sense of period do make a difference, but a similar meeting in modern surroundings should perhaps be staged in a way to discourage children falling into instant trust of strangers.

A programme maker needs to be aware of the likely views of the audience — and especially in the context of the current news. The attitude of the British public to guns was affected considerably at the time of the 'Hungerford Massacre' in Berkshire and there are numerous other, almost daily events like arson, joy-riding, bombings, which *must* be taken into consideration lest they have an association in the audience's mind in relation to the television programme on which you expend your labour, care and energy.

Whatever happened to innocence?

NOTES

1. My own 'interest', here, is that of a practising Christian, which I hope informs my attitude to my work, but which would not lead me to abuse other faiths — nor to promote them.

2. *Violence on Television*, The Report of the Wyatt Committee (1987), and *Guidelines for Production Staff* (BBC, 1987). There is also a book on the subject, *Violence and the Media* (BBC Books, 1988).

3. *Television is good for your Kids*, pp.159 ff.

4. The exception here was the fine series directed by Colin Cant and produced by Paul Stone of *The Machine Gunners,* a book by the late Robert Westall.

The Future

I have considered some of the things that may happen to children's programming in the future, not all of which looks very bright. The dangers seem to take a variety of forms:

- There may be a diminishing lack of commitment to originate 'quality' programmes of all types for children by some distributors.

- With proliferation of outlets, there could be a dilution of available talent, at least until a new pool of talent has gained some experience.

- There is a pressure from advertisers to push for bigger audiences, which have control over money (this excludes many children).

- Financial pressures on broadcasters, which might mean the spread of short contracts for programme staff. This could dilute the pool of talent and destroy the specialised base of children's programming developed over many years.

- The entire concept of the worth of children's programmes is under intermittent attack. In the future, some of these attacks may be severe enough to wound.

Offsetting some of these gloomy predictions is the interesting possibility of a continent-wide — even a worldwide — network (or networks) with a pooling of resources to provide a wider variety of material than that currently available in any one nation. The flaw in this is that more power would reside in fewer hands and that, across the continent, or across the world, there would be an overall reduction in variety. There would be less scope for the individual, the parochial (or National), and the quirky or more controversial material. Each country would veto anything it did not like — the result might be inoffensive to fifteen nations — and ineffectual.

In America there is the *Action for Children's Television Campaign*, and its counterpart here, the *British Action for Children's Television Campaign*. These are non-political bodies aiming in the U.S. to restore quality and variety to children's programmes, and in this country, to maintain — or improve — the quality and variety.

Children deserve the best we can give them in television because the future is theirs. Children's television, therefore, is a richly rewarding area in which to work. The audience renews itself and is always fresh in a way that no other audience can be.

I have heard people say that they have lived through the Golden Age of Children's Television. Perhaps this is because memory always tends to make the past rosier than reality.

It is up to you to give viewers another 'Golden Age' simply "because it *is* worthwhile".